Bedlam
Without Bars
A Fanciful Dixie Peep Show

"These venerable Virginia ruins..." *(see p. 62)*

Bedlam Without Bars
A Fanciful Dixie Peep Show

GEORGE HOLBERT TUCKER

Illustrated by the Author

"For what do we live, but to make sport for our neighbors, and laugh at them in our turn."

Mr. Bennet,
in Jane Austen's
PRIDE AND PREJUDICE

HAMPTON ROADS
PUBLISHING COMPANY, INC.

Also by GEORGE HOLBERT TUCKER

Norfolk City Marriage Bonds (1797-1850)
Tidewater Landfalls
More Tidewater Landfalls
Norfolk Highlights (1584-1881)
Virginia Supernatural Tales
A Goodly Heritage: A History of Jane Austen's Family
The Jane Austen Companion (contributor)
Cavalier Saints and Sinners

For information, write:

Hampton Roads Publishing Co., Inc.
891 Norfolk Square
Norfolk, VA 23502

Or call: 804-459-2453
    FAX: 804-455-8907

If this book is unavailable from your local bookseller, it may be obtained directly from the publisher. Call toll-free 1-800-766-8009 (orders only).

ISBN 1-878901-23-0

10 9 8 7 6 5 4 3 2 1

Printed in the United States of America

These are true and uncensored tales
of life between 1900 and 1950
in the Virginia port city
I choose to call Queensport.
The names have been changed
to protect the innocent,
and the guilty.
But it all happened.

For Elizabeth

CONTENTS

Bedlam Without Bars:

A Fanciful Dixie Peep-Show

"If it was comfortable enough for Robert E. Lee . . ."

1. The Lay of the Land

Having lived in this zany world for over eighty years, there is only one thing of which I am absolutely certain—the human comedy is a hardy perennial. That being the case, let me emphasize that the following anecdotal chronicle of Queensport, the southern bedlam without bars where I have conducted most of my research, will not be a sentimental sashay down memory lane.

In case you are beginning to wonder where Queensport is, permit me to offer a suggestion as well as a clue. As for the suggestion, let me warn you that you will be wasting your time if you try to track it down on any map of the United States, ancient or modern. The clue is more important, for if you have ever been subjected to history warped by nostalgia, particularly of the moonlight and magnolia variety, you will realize without reading much further that Queensport could only have existed in that Cloud-Cuckoo-Land south of the Mason and Dixon Line known as the Old Dominion.

Now that these two important points have been settled, let me urge you to relax and allow me to conduct you down the rabbit hole of memory to another time and place which existed between the turn of the present century and the bombardment of Pearl Harbor when progress, spelled with a Capital P, was still regarded throughout the Southland as the primary tenet of Mammon's creed.

Even though I hate to admit it, I am not a Simon-pure Queensporter, having been born a few years before the sinking of the Titanic in a nearby one-horse town where the favorite hobby of the natives was hoarding Confederate money against the time when the South would stage its Second Coming. When I was twelve, however, my father felt the need for wider horizons for his family, at which time he chose Queensport as our next destination.

Although the move considerably broadened my vista of the human comedy, I quickly perceived that the bittersweet miasma of defeat that had hovered over my birthplace was just as prevalent in Queensport, although it operated on a more dedicated level than the mere stashing of Confederate shinplasters in a shoe box. What is more, I soon learned that any Queensporter who did not subscribe to the dogma that God had voluntarily abdicated in favor of General Robert E. Lee when the latter entered Valhalla automatically found himself persona non grata before he could whistle the first bars of "Dixie" to prove his Southern fidelity.

To illustrate the point, there was this tale concerning Queensport's oldest Episcopal church, which had been visited on at least one occasion by none other than the chief saint in the Confederate hagiography. At a considerably later date, a naval officer and his wife, both Yankees by birth, had been invited to attend a wedding there, but upon arriving discovered the church was so crowded they had to sit in a stuffy balcony. As the woman in the party had not anticipated this seating arrangement, she had not brought along a fan.

After a fruitless search in the pew for something to raise a breeze, she fell back on an envelope from her purse to keep the air in circulation. While frantically attempting to dispel the heat, she turned to an elderly spinster sitting beside her and remarked, "My God! This place is like an oven!" Looking down her nose at the latter-day carpetbagger, the Southern vestal snapped, "If it was comfortable enough for Robert E. Lee, it should be comfortable enough for anyone - *including you!*"

To return to my own particular onward and upward struggle, as my ancestral loyalties had been with the North in 1861-65, that was a major strike against me. My harking from a mill town that had mushroomed after "de Wah" with the aid of Yankee capital was an additional social detriment, for Queensporters of all classes had a tendency to scorn anyone with Northern connections, much less a person whose life had formerly been regulated by blasts of a mill whistle.

Even so, I managed to fend off the rebel wolves by keeping my eyes and ears open and my mouth shut, a policy which succeeded in diverting the spotlight from me most of the time. Meanwhile, I soon discovered my precarious perch on the lowest rung of the Queensport social ladder gave me a unique view of the Achilles' heels of my self-styled betters, an observation which ultimately worked to my advantage. Once my Confederate-besotted townsmen realized the embarrassing opportunities my humbler, but advantageous, position afforded, they figured it was wiser to move over and share a place with me on the upper rung rather than risk further mortification.

Of course, if you were anybody in Queensport, you were automatically an Episcopalian, an assertion that the following anecdote will substantiate. On one occasion the 12-year-old daughter of one of the town's leading Anglicans accompanied a Baptist playmate to a revival at the latter's church. After holding forth on hell and damnation for some time in the pulpit, the preacher got so carried away he stepped down from the rostrum and began pacing up and down the aisles exhorting those present to embrace Salvation.

Hoping to drum up trade for the Master by using the "little child shall lead them" tactic, he paused, placed his hands on the Anglican girl's curly head and enquired unctuously, "Child, are you a Christian?" There was brief moment of silence, then the moppet replied emphatically, "No, sir, I'm an Episcopalian!"

As most Queensport Episcopalians were formerly noted for their enjoyment of the good things of this life, including the pleasures of the bottle, while preparing for the dubious ones of the next, it was a truth universally acknowledged, as Jane Austen wittily expressed it, that where four of them were gathered together there was always a *fifth*. Another upper crust Queensport article of faith also maintained that when a Baptist had learned to write he automatically became a Methodist, while any Methodist who could afford to buy flour by the barrel straightway put a cast iron elk in his front yard and joined the Episcopal Church.

As for those Baptists who yearned for respectability in the arms of the latter-day disciples of John Wesley, they were no threat to the Queensport status quo. But the affluent flour-by-the-barrel Methodists, who were straining at the bit to exchange Amazing Grace for the more exclusive climate of Anglicanism, were the real problem. As time passed, the upward thrust of that particular platoon of onward Christian soldiers, with their eyes firmly fixed on the upper rungs of the social ladder, particularly membership in the snobbish Episcopal-dominated Queensport Cotillion Club, made it increasingly difficult for the Old Guard to maintain its traditional battle lines.

To illustrate the latter's combat tactics, on one occasion when the spotlight was being concentrated on the obscure origins of a *nouveau riche* menage, a young woman at a party turned to an elderly member of her family, a pompadoured Buddha wearing a jewelled band around her neck, and gushed, "Why, grandmother remembers they ate off red oilcloth when they first came to Queensport," adding, "Don't you, grandmother?" Without looking up from her needlepoint, the old lady raised a knowing eyebrow and settled the point with noncommittal finality. "Now, Melissa," she admonished, "at my age you mustn't embarrass me before company by requiring me to recall the exact color."

After that mellifluous tuberose-scented barb, almost anything would have been an anticlimax, but before beginning this memoir I would like to share one more anecdote to illustrate the social atmosphere that gave the Queensport of the past its unique tone.

At a reception sponsored by the Mockingbird Camellia Society, a self-satisfied guest swept up to one of the hostesses and observed, "Do you know, Belle, if Our Lord visited Queensport, I doubt if He could mix in our sphere of society." Without batting an eye, the hostess replied smugly, "Oh, no, my dear, you're wrong. I believe you've forgotten how well connected He was on His Father's side!"

" . . . *winding up with Yankee Doodle*"

2. Patriotic Rungs on the Social Ladder

Social status in the Queensport of my youth was regulated by the degree of prestige attached to whatever patriotic societies with which the women of one's family had managed to affiliate themselves. If a postulant could prove her descent from a Colonial bigwig (even if he had arrived in the New World under the most unfavorable circumstances) and could also obtain the sponsorship of two already anointed members, she might eventually be admitted to the rarified realm presided over by the town's top drawer flag-waving group known as the Founders.

For those too timid to run the gantlet of snobbish approval or others smarting from having been rejected from the sacrosanct portal guarded by the Founders, there was the less exclusive group known as the Colonizers, membership in which gave one a quasi-socially acceptable position. Even so, the Founders and the Colonizers, who carried on a constant warfare over which group constituted the First Families of Virginia, encountered occasional rebuffs as the following pertinent anecdote will show.

During World War I a Queensport-born Army officer married a highly literate French girl while he was overseas. Shortly after the couple returned to the United States they were given a welcome home dinner party, at which a tiresome Queensport ancestor-conscious matron bragged on and on concerning her early Virginia forebears. Feeling that the newcomer from France was not sufficiently impressed, she turned to her and remarked, "I don't suppose you understand what an FFV is?" To this, the Paris-born bride replied archly, "Oh, yes

I do. You see I have just finished reading Defoe's 'Moll Flanders!'"

The next rung down on the socio-spread-eagle ladder was formerly occupied by the Patriots whose meetings in Queensport were always opened with a collective hands-on-ample-bosoms dual pledge of allegiance to the American flag and a framed fragment of a mourning shawl of dubious authenticity reputed to have been worn by Martha Washington. Membership in the Patriots automatically presupposed two things. First, you had to be a certified descendant of someone who had served, even briefly, against the British, a requirement that occasionally resulted in absurdity. For instance, one matron proudly proclaimed her descent from a Colonial ne'er-do-well who had officiated for one week only as a "sentry of the cesspit" for the Virginia Militia just before Cornwallis surrendered at Yorktown to the tune of "The World Turned Upside Down."

The other requirement for membership in the Patriots was suspicion of everything happening in the contemporary world. This latter stipulation was once hilariously highlighted in the following newspaper account of a meeting of the Queensport conclave, the last sentence of which unintentionally attributed an improbable performance to the hostess for the occasion.

> After a stirring meeting, during which the United Nations and Eleanor Roosevelt were roundly denounced as definitely not being in accord with the Patriots' conception of high American ideals, Mrs. _____ entertained her sister members at a Lucullan tea and coffee repast in the dining room of her stately home. Mrs. ____'s elegant silver service was placed at one end of her mahogany groaning board and her gold decorated Sevres china tea set adorned the other extremity of the same polished expanse. In honor of the occasion, Mrs. ____, who wore a large straw hat decorated with red, white and blue cornflowers, poured generously from both ends.

Although the gradations of the Queensport social ladder, from the top rung occupied by the Founders to the Patriots' perch two steps below, were fiercely guarded from interlopers, the fourth bar down, garrisoned by the Varina Howell Davis Chapter of the Southern Valkyries (familiarly known as the SVs), was wide open territory for any woman whose immediate male antecedents had cast their lot with the Southland either from misguided idealism or from a desire to relieve the boredom of marital existence.

The war cry of the Queensport SVs, by far the most jingoistic group in town, was "What! Shake hands above the bloody chasm! Never!" Moreover, some of the more militant members were reputed to have owned chamber pots, the interior bottoms of which were adorned with likenesses of either General William Tecumseh Sherman or General Benjamin Franklin ("Beast") Butler.

Also, unlike the other Queensport patriotic ladies, the SVs had their own clubhouse, the walls of which were adorned with lurid daubs of the battle between the Merrimack and the Monitor, the efforts of a third-rate sign painter, a grandfather of one of the more bellicose members who been reluctantly admitted to the fringes of Queensport society only because her ancestor had been a coal heaver on the celebrated Confederate ironclad.

To be tainted with Yankee ancestry was a sin against the Holy Ghost as far as the SVs were concerned, and the forebears of anyone with a claim to respectability who took up residence in Queensport was automatically subjected to a microscopic genealogical examination before being declared socially acceptable.

For instance, there was this tale concerning a family that moved into a high-toned Queensport neighborhood during World War I. The newcomers were obviously genteel, but the matrons of the area (all unreconstructed SVs) hesitated to visit them as there was no indication of how they regarded The Late Unpleasantness.

Finally the nosiest of the SVs broke the ice and paid the new family a formal afternoon call. Shortly after leaving their house, she sounded the tocsin and there was an immediate gathering in her parlor around the sherry decanter. After a dramatic pause, the woman announced, "It will be perfectly proper to visit them, girls! All of their male family portraits are wearing gray uniforms!"

There were also a couple of other related yarns of the same nature which should be included if for no other reason than to indicate that an unquestioned belief in the justification of the Southern War for Independence was not only a primary Queensport act of faith, it was also on the same dogmatic wavelength as the Apostles' Creed.

The first tale concerned two Queensport "maiden ladies," both charter members of the Varina Howell Davis Chapter of the SVs, who were enjoying a glass of sherry with equally certified Southern friends one New Year's Day when a recently married apostate cousin and his Northern bride were seen approaching the house. Catching a glimpse of the enemy through the starched lace parlor curtains, the more vocal sister hissed, "Quick, Lorena, lock up that sherry in the sideboard (pronounced "sidebode" in Queensport) and get out the dandelion wine. That should be good enough for any damned Yankee!"

The other anecdote involved another unreconstructed SV who returned home from a trip to Washington where she was horrified to discover that Arlington, the former home as well as the burial place of the Custis and Lee families, was being used as a national cemetery. "Good God, I shudder to think how those Southern aristocrats will feel on Judgement Day," she snorted. "Poor souls, can't you imagine their reaction when they rise from their graves and find themselves surrounded by Yankee soldiers!"

The irreverent in Queensport could always count on the newspaper accounts of the SVs for a laugh. For example, one long-winded story of a gathering ended thus: "Before the meeting adjourned, Miss ____ opened her dulcet-toned rosewood melodeon and warbled 'I'm a Good Old Rebel,' 'The Yellow Rose of Texas,' and several other Confederate canticles as a heartfelt tribute to the Lost Cause." Even so, the SVs of my boyhood didn't always have things their way, for there was one memorable occasion when they met with a well-deserved, latter-day Appomattox.

The victor in that particular post-Civil War skirmish was a respectable spinster, the daughter of a former Federal colonel who had participated in Sherman's March to the Sea. The woman and her father, a widower and an official of a Northern firm, had moved to Queensport early in the twentieth century when his company opened an office there. Neither father nor daughter, in view of their connection with the winning side of The War of the Rebellion, was popular. But that didn't trouble them. Being financially independent and liking one another's company sufficiently to disregard the cold shoulders of their neighbors, they lived harmoniously together until the Grim Reaper finally removed the father to the great Union campground in the sky.

After that the spinster led a sheltered life, sharing her friendship with a few unbiased acquaintances, tending her flower garden, and sitting in lone, upright elegance on Sundays in her well-quarantined pew in the Episcopal church of which she was a member. Even so, the Queensport SVs still resented the fact that her father had marched with Sherman, and contrary to the reputed refinement of Southern gentlewomen, they developed the bad habit of referring to her as "the daughter of that damned Yankee," often within earshot. Instead of striking back, however, the woman bided her time, and the good Lord, who reputedly answers the prayers of the oppressed, presumably arranged the battleground on which she routed her persecutors.

In those days the Queensport SVs held an annual Memorial Day soiree at the home of one of their members. These occasions, plentifully supplied with traditional Southern delicacies, were always enhanced by the "silver-tongued oratory" of some gentleman qualified by Confederate connections to attempt to add an extra leaf to the already crowded laurels circling the brows of Marse Robert and Stonewall Jackson. That year the meeting took place in the home of one of Queensport's most unreconstructed female rebels, directly across the street from the spinster's home.

Armed with that knowledge, the latter formulated her battle plans. An accomplished pianist, she was the only person in Queensport who possessed a piano equipped with a banjo pedal, an attachment capable of making the instrument sound like the uninhibited performance of an endman in a minstrel show. Having the piano moved near the open front windows of her parlor, she adjusted the banjo pedal for a maximum of musical mayhem, then sat and waited.

The party across the street got under way and in no time the speaker's eulogy of The Lost Cause was booming through the windows, flung open in those pre-air-conditioned days to catch any stray breeze. At that point the spinster swung into action.

Beginning with a stirring rendition of "The Star Spangled Banner," she launched into a clangorous recital of Yankee musical favorites including "The Battle Hymn of the Republic," "Tramp, Tramp, Tramp, the Boys Are Marching," "When Johnny Comes Marching Home," and "The Battle Cry of Freedom," winding up with "Yankee Doodle" and "Marching Through Georgia," with all the trimmings.

Before that musical bombardment of the songs that had carried the Boys in Blue to victory, the Queensport SVs were forced to acknowledge that their thin gray line was completely outnumbered and outmaneuvered. Also, when the only Union veteran living in the neighborhood, who was sitting on his front porch, yelled, "Yippee! Play 'em all over again", the SVs surrendered unconditionally, realizing that a stillness similar to that which prevailed at Appomattox after Marse Robert's capitulation was their only recourse.

3. Gremlins in the Newsroom

Any newspaper capable of coming up with a page one, bold type headline proclaiming: "Queensport Pussy Judged Best In South" deserved a prize. That *double entendre* actually appeared in the *Bugle*, Queensport's evening journal, after aleurophiles from all over Dixie had participated in a widely publicized cat show at the city armory a few years after the Armistice ended World War I.

Actually, Queensport formerly had two newspapers, the *Courier*, the city's older and more conservative morning journal, and the *Bugle*, the afternoon news vehicle which featured more diverse pictorial coverage and sensational stories as a sop to the ragtag and bobtail. Any family with any pretensions to gentility subscribed to the *Courier*. For its sacrosanct journalistic podium was deemed the only proper place from which the births, engagements, weddings and obituaries of the quality could be announced for the first time.

To cite an example, a well-known dowager *in extremis* telephoned the obituary editor of the *Courier* from her hospital bed hoping to be able to dictate the details of her death notice in advance. When she was told he was away on a two-day fishing trip, she sighed, then said, "Well, I'll try to hold out until he gets back." She made it, too, for after dictating her obituary notice two days later to the returned journalist, she died that evening, after which her relations had the satisfaction of knowing that her passing had been initially announced in the *Courier*.

The *Courier's* protocol was not foolproof, however, for both the society and obituary editors of the *Bugle* were eagle-eyed in their vigilance to scoop their rivals on the *Courier*. When that happened, there were long faces in the

"Queesnport Pussy Judged Best In South"

Courier's newsroom comparable to those affected by earlier upper-class Queensporters when the news of Lee's surrender at Appomattox became public.

This time-honored tradition has changed now, for any rivalry existing between the *Courier* and the *Bugle* ended when the two journals merged some time ago. That being the case, I'd like to hark back to the era before the merger to share a few memorable examples of rococo journalistic prose, misprints, howlers and *double entendre* headlines which appeared in both papers before computers banished the gremlins of mischance as well as rank individuality from Queensport's two earlier newsrooms.

Both papers formerly suffered from an overdose of Confederate bias as well as hothouse journalistic verbosity, as this excerpt from a turn-of-the-century wedding announcement from the *Courier* will illustrate. In touting the pedigree of the groom, the society editor gushed:

> Oh his maternal side, one of his great-grandsires sacrificed his spotless young manhood on the altar of the Southland when he sallied forth like Ivanhoe of old to defend the ever-glorious Confederacy from the more recent counterparts of the hordes of Attila the Hun.

To give the *Bugle* equal billing, its society editor really pulled out all of the stops when she composed this journalistic *allegro con brio* describing a party for a prospective debutante a few years after World War I:

> Mr. and Mrs. ____ entertained last evening at their family mansion with an end-of-school terpsichorean entertainment in honor of their lovely granddaughter, the bedimpled, azure-eyed Miss ____, who was recently voted the best Charleston dancer at Evelyn Byrd Preparatory School.
>
> The honored and distinguished guests were received in the spacious hallway, the scene of revelry by night of several generations of the family, which was decorated with pink and green crepe paper streamers suspended from the crystal chandeliers that have illumined the radiant countenances of many a beau and

belle in their day. Placed conspicuously in the hallway was a large three-tiered birthday cake decorated with miniature Stars and Bars, but given a contemporary touch by being topped with a spun sugar statuette of Clara Bow, the "the It Girl."

After partaking an elegant collation, the party moved to the mimosa-scented portico where out-of-town guests joined the others in an evening of tripping the light fantastic. Such a good time was had by all that everyone was reluctant to leave when the tall grandfather clock on the spiral stairway boomed out the Cinderella hour of midnight.

To turn to the howlers, there was one word which early became taboo on the *Courier* after the ordinarily sharp-eyed proofreaders failed to detect the following Freudian slip in a report of a prestigious wedding: "After the ceremony the groom treated the guests to a cockout on the lawn of his parents' home."

This was bad enough, but when an announcement of festivities following another wedding reported, "The conception was held on the mezzanine floor of the ____ Hotel," there was literally weeping, wailing and gnashing of teeth. Even so, a sardonic staff member saved the day, for the newsroom at least, when he remarked, "It must have been damned hard on the bride's back!"

These were beauts, but there were others. For instance, the *Bugle* once announced that a prominent matron had been "the fortunate winner of twelve free greasings" in a contest held by a local service station. Then there was the time when the same paper proclaimed that the Queensport Women's Christian Temperance Union had departed "in a fleet of buses for a spiritual retreat at Endless Taverns."

At another time, the front page obituary of one of Queensport's most notorious womanizers, also a Confederate veteran, contained this unintentional Freudianism: "He was personally commended by Gen. Robert E. Lee for shamelessly exposing himself at the Battle of Seven Pines." Also in the same category was this slip perpetrated by the *Courier*. In announcing an Easter matinee for the Queensport elderly at a local theater, the reporter ended his story thus: "Every Senior Citizen who lays an egg in the doorman's hand will be admitted free."

Then there were the *double entendre* headlines, unpremeditated or otherwise, which provided a constant source of entertainment for the prurient minded. For example, there was a Queensport lady gardener who had devoted a good deal of time and money to preserving a rose bush that had been grown from a cutting taken from a wreath that had adorned "Stonewall" Jackson's grave at the time of his burial. When a story praising her efforts appeared in a Garden Week supplement of the *Courier*, it was headed: "Miss _____ Treasures Her Old Bush."

Then there was the time when a notoriously straitlaced Queensport matron was the subject of a feature article during the Christmas season since she had concocted several unique ornaments of wax and mistletoe to hang from the chandeliers in her hall. All would have been well, except the *Bugle* published a six-column cut of the grim-visaged woman holding one of her creations bearing the cutline: "Kissing Balls Her Specialty."

That was minor, however, by comparison with what follows. During the era when Franklin D. Roosevelt was president and money to combat polio was raised at publicly sponsored dances, the *Courier* brazenly announced: "President's Balls Will Be Held Simultaneously In Two Queensport Areas Tonight."

But the gem of them all appeared in the *Bugle*. When a restored pipe organ in one of the city's oldest churches was rededicated by a local musician who also happened to be one of Queensport's better-known nymphomaniacs, the story was headed: "Ancient Organ Came Alive Under Her Talented Touch."

"*Well, get it over with . . .*"

4. The Ritual of Bending the Elbow

Bending the elbow, in moderation or to excess, was the one long-standing Queensport tradition that successfully withstood the onslaughts of the Women's Christian Temperance Union and other forms of killjoyism over the years.

That the tradition was deeply rooted is illustrated by this pre-Prohibition yarn concerning a group of Queensport sports who came to the conclusion in a semi-sober moment that they were hitting the bottle so freely they felt the necessity of taking the pledge.

"Wait a minute," the more cynical of the prospective pledge-takers mused, "What are we going to do if a friend drops by the house and we offer him a sociable drink? We just can't sit there and let him drink alone, you know."

Well, that's true," the others agreed. "We'll allow that exception."

"Then what are we going to do if we drop in on a friend and he offers us a drink? You know it wouldn't be polite to refuse."

"That's right," the others reflected. "That will also have to be taken into consideration."

"And just imagine walking into the Old Dominion Club and seeing all of our friends enjoying their afternoon toddies and not be able to join in," the questioner continued.

"Good God! that would be a calamity!" the others assented. "We must certainly make an exception for the club."

"Then consider what would happen if one of us was strolling down the street and was invited by a friend to join him for a drink in a public bar," the cynic continued.

"Oh yes, that's right," the others agreed. "That exception will also have to be considered."

At that point one of the crowd suggested they quit while they were ahead. After that they drew up and signed the following statement:

We, the undersigned, realizing the evils of drink, have decided to take the pledge to imbibe no more except under the following circumstances:

1. In our own homes when offering a drink to a friend.
2. In the home of a friend when offered a drink.
3. At the Old Dominion Club at all times.
4. In any duly licensed bar.

It was at the Old Dominion Club that Queensport's most memorable toasting session took place. At a banquet attended by prominent Virginians and North Carolinians, a tipsy carrot-topped son of the Tar Heel State arose and proposed:

Here's to North Carolina
With her wonderful birds of prey;
They fly over old Virginia
And crap on her every day!

In reply, an equally inebriated but loyal son of the Old Dominion replied:

Here's to old Virginia;
Why, her soil is so fertile and rich,
You can keep your turds from your wonderful birds;
You red-headed son of a bitch!

The Old Dominion Club was also the setting for still another Queensport bibulous yarn. One evening before the advent of Prohibition a notorious local lush topped his usual record by consuming an astronomical number of highballs at the town's elite watering hole. Hours later, when one of his female companions missed him at another party, she telephoned the bartender at the club and inquired frantically if he had seen her three-sheets-in-the-wind companion. To this query, the bartender chuckled and replied, "Lawd, ma'am, I ain't swept up yet."

Fondness for the bottle generated quite a few other Queensport bacchanalian legends, and strange as it may seem some of the best of them had one or another of the town's churches as an unlikely backdrop. For instance, there was one prominent town drunk who never turned up at his particular Episcopal church except on Communion Sundays, on which occasions he was one of the first to advance somewhat unsteadily to the altar rail when the time came for partaking of the elements.

Leaving nothing to chance, he would reach out and grab the chalice from the rector when his time to quaff arrived, after which his resounding "Ahhhhh!!!!!" of content caused the devout to quake in their shoes for fear of immediate Divine Retribution.

Then there was this tale of a Queensport father and his pert little daughter who were attending Holy Communion together at the same church. All went well until the time came to approach the altar rail for participation in the Eucharist, at which time the father, who had a serious alcoholic problem, told his daughter she would have to remain behind in the pew, adding he would explain the reason later.

After he had returned from partaking the Sacrament, the little girl was insistent that he tell her the reason immediately. When he hissed "Shhhhh!!!!!" in her direction, she gave him a knowing look, then wailed, "You've been boozing again, and mama's not going to like it a bit!"

There was another occasion during the Prohibition era when a witty Queensport clergyman was solemnizing a marriage, during which a groomsman slipped out into the vestibule to take a swig of bootleg whiskey from a flask he had secreted in his overcoat pocket. Unfortunately, he was well on his way to a severe case of *delirium tremens* and he dropped the bottle.

In no time the rank odor of corn liquor not only permeated the church but reached the nostrils of the officiating clergyman. Pausing for a moment, he lifted his eyes heavenward and remarked, "Lord have mercy! I've often heard of the odor of sanctity, but this is the first time I've ever smelled it!"

On another occasion during a revival at a Baptist church a hellfire and damnation evangelist was holding forth before a capacity congregation on the terrors of the Day of Judgment. As he waxed increasingly eloquent, his clarion tones attracted the attention of a tipsy citizen who was staggering homeward. His curiosity was so aroused he walked into the church and took a seat in a back pew. At the climax of his sermon, the preacher cried out, "And in that day, brethren, the sheep will be on the right hand and the goats will be on the left." Then, raising his voice even higher, he demanded rhetorically, "Who will be the goats?" Receiving no response from the congregation, he repeated the question in an even louder voice.

That time he made his point, for the drunk rose from his seat and reeled unsteadily down the aisle to the mourners' bench. Looking up at the preacher, he announced, "You're putting on a Goddamned good show! Rather than see it fizzle out for a lack of volunteers, I'll be the goat!"

To consider Demon rum outside the limits of Queensport's sacred precincts, there was this yarn concerning a prominent citizen who devoted most of his waking hours to the bottle. The man's tippling was so constant, however, that it caused little comment until he staggered home late one Saturday night, woke up his household, and threatened to commit suicide.

For an hour or so afterward the air was loud with his ravings and the frantic pleas of his family that he desist. Finally everyone in the neighborhood had been aroused and expected momentarily to hear the blast that would end his life. When that didn't materialize, a spirited matron who lived next door to the drunk decided she had finally had enough. Finding his front door open, she entered and walked into the dining room, the scene of the ongoing fracas.

"What did you say you are going to do?" she asked coolly.

"I'm going to blow my brains out," the boozer ranted.

"All right, then," the woman continued, "where do you keep your pistol?"

Looking somewhat surprised, the toper pointed unsteadily toward a sideboard drawer. Taking him completely off his guard, the matron yanked open the drawer, took out the gun, and laid it on the dining room table.

"Well, get it over with," she demanded. "Decent people around here are sick and tired of your low-life doings."

Confronted in that manner, the booze artist straightened up and glowered at his adversary. Then he provided Queensport with its most memorable quote for that particular year. "The hell I will!" he bellowed. "What do you take me for - a Goddamned fool?"

". . . operated by French Lil"

5. Red-Light District Hailed Confederacy

Queensport's red-light district, which formerly occupied several blocks of substantial property in the older section of the city, was a time-honored exhaust valve for the sexually uninhibited until it was abolished by the combined forces of militant local Puritanism and the Army, Navy and Marine Corps after the Japanese attack on Pearl Harbor.

Realistic old-time politicians, acting on the inherited wisdom of those who had gone before them, had always taken a liberal attitude toward Queensport's sexual Elysian Fields. Until they were wiped out by the first upsurge of the killjoys who later proclaimed themselves the Moral Majority, however, the politicos were content to let well enough alone so long as the bordello keepers paid their taxes and those who plied their trade there stayed off the streets and gamboled with their paying partners behind closed doors.

Even so, Queensport's Paphian area proved a problem on one memorable occasion, and it was not until a good deal of soul-searching had taken place that a suitable solution of the situation was reached. The impasse was brought about when a headier-then-usual wave of chauvinistic Confederate fervor prompted the Southern Valkyries to mark every spot in the city associated with The Lost Cause.

All went well until it was discovered that the first Confederate flag that had ever taken the Queensport breeze had been flown from a window of a still active whorehouse originally operated by a long-deceased madam known as French Lil. Historical evidence revealed that immediately after the bombardment of Fort Sumter in 1861 several of Lil's customers had taken a recess from their more intimate and enjoyable pleasures and had unfurled the Stars and Bars from a second story window of her establishment.

Where the flag had come from remained a mystery, but as it was certain the event had taken place, there was a stalemate until the latter-day rebels belonging to the memorial committee compromised by setting up a commemorative marker just outside the limits of the red-light district.

This bore a legend beginning with: "Two blocks to the eastward, the first Confederate flag was publicly exhibited in Queensport. . . ." The solution worked perfectly until some wag blocked out the first letter "l" in "publicly," thereby giving added point to the circumstances necessitating the erection of the plaque elsewhere.

Like all other areas of its kind, Queensport's bower of carnality had its folk heroes, one of the more memorable of whom, a latter-day satyr known as Good Time Charlie, belonged to one of the town's most distinguished families. A portly, jovial bachelor, Charlie also was the animated Queensport art gallery of his era, practically every inch of his body being covered with explicit tattoos.

For instance, according to the evidence of the embalmer who prepared his body for burial, Charlie's ample chest, the nipples of which were presided over by twin bluebirds and were labeled "Sweet" and "Sour" respectively, bore a motto in Old English letters proclaiming, "Your Soul May Belong To Jesus, But Your Ass Belongs To Me."

Beneath that emblazonment, Charlie's rotund bay window was adorned with a spirited depiction of a red-coated hunting party on horseback with the hounds in full cry in pursuit of a fox, the brush of whose tail the artist had been careful to depict disappearing into the cleft of Charlie's well-upholstered buttocks.

Unlike his peers, who had long since exchanged single erotic bliss for bit-in-the-teeth Holy Wedlock, Charlie continued to take his pleasures where he found them until he died "in the saddle" of a heart attack in a posh Storyville brothel while attending the Mardi Gras in New Orleans just before the outbreak of World War I. When the news of his death reached Queensport, a delegation of sorrowing madams and a few of his more intimate cronies met the train that brought his body back from the Crescent City for burial.

One madam, a particular friend of the deceased, asked for permission to visit the house where his coffin had been taken in order to gaze on his familiar countenance for the last time. After a hasty conference, Charlie's family agreed to permit the "viewing," as the ceremony was then referred to in Queensport's obituary columns, but they specified she must come heavily veiled at midnight in order to do so. These stipulations were indignantly rejected by the madam, who bided her time and planned her revenge.

The first shot in the fray was fired when she and her doxies commemorated the sad event by ordering an enormous memorial wreath of red roses, the ribbon streamer of which bore a prominent gold-lettered motto: "For Darling Charlie - In Remembrance of Things Past - From His Many Light O'Loves."

After this floral tribute had been placed near the gravesite and had been memorized for speedy dissemination by those attending the funeral, the large crowd which had gathered for the last rites was surprised by the arrival of three touring cars, overflowing with the more celebrated denizens of Charlie's favorite habitat, all of them wearing fashionable mourning and carrying oversized black-bordered pocket handkerchiefs. Naturally, Charlie's family was upset by this invasion, but the climax was yet to come.

Knowing Charlie had been sweet on a merry widow who lived in a nearby city, the madam had wired her the news of his death, urging her to join the contingent of red-light district mourners. The train was late, however, so the widow was unable to arrive on time to accompany the madam and her girls to the cemetery. But that did not stop her from attending the funeral.

Just as the preacher was about to commit Charlie's immortal soul to his Maker, a taxi chugged through the wrought iron gates of the cemetery and sped to the area where the funeral party was assembled. At that point the tardy widow leaped from the taxi screaming, "He's mine! He's mine! Don't take him away from me!," after which she shouldered her way through the astonished crowd and leaped into the grave. Then, before all hell broke loose, an eagle-eyed female mourner shrieked, "My God! That huzzy is wearing red silk garters and no *bloomers!*"

That episode really rocked the town down to its goody-goody moorings, but there was still another Queensport bawdy-house story that topped the widow's performance.

A few years after Good Time Charlie was laid to rest, the madam of one of the town's more elegant brothels went to the president of Queensport's leading bank and applied for a loan of fifteen thousand dollars, saying she needed it to refurbish her establishment. The banker, who was one of the madam's more discreet carriage trade customers, was perfectly willing to advance the money, but he advised her to take it on a long-term loan since the interest would not be as prohibitive as that which a short-term note would entail. The woman refused to do business that way, however, and the banker finally agreed to lend her the money on her own terms, even going so far as to place his name on the note as her security.

Three months later the madam returned, but instead of paying the first installment on the note as the banker anticipated, she pulled out a roll of bills and settled the transaction in full. Taking time out to polish his rimless glasses, the banker finally commented, "You'll have to admit my advice was sound, for if you had done what I advised, this wouldn't have cost you as much in the end."

There was a pause, during which the madam took out her vanity case and powdered her nose. Then she gave the banker a sly wink and quipped, "Well, you see, I knew the All-State Fair and the Shriners' Convention were coming to Queensport this year, but damned if I knew we'd be getting the Methodist Conference at the same time."

"I'm turning the other cheek"

6. Culture -
Pierian Spring Club Style

Culture in Queensport was formerly championed by the now defunct Pierian Spring Club made up largely of alumnae from the Mary Custis Lee Female Seminary, the area's most prestigious "finishing school," where belle-oriented blandishments rather than serious studies were accorded stellar priorities in the curriculum.

Even if a member had not attended that particular institution, affiliation with the Pierians constituted a tremendous social advantage. Apart from serving as an aesthetic exhaust valve for those who felt the necessity to burn with a pure and gemlike flame, it gave the less dedicated an unrivaled opportunity to show off their latest millinery while dozing through high-toned lectures or musicals before enjoying a cup of tea, several petit fours and an exhilarating gossip session later on.

Unlike Queensport's more militant Southern Valkyries, whose tatty homes were prominently adorned with anemic watercolor renditions of Confederate battle flags and whose literary flights rarely soared higher than pious meditations on Father Abram Joseph Ryan's "The Sword of Robert E. Lee," the Pierians' houses were usually distinctive for their chintzy comfort, highlighted by oak-framed sepia Perry prints of Corot landscapes, George Frederick Watts's "Hope," and Sir Anthony Van Dyck's "Baby Stuart." The Pierians' choice of literature was also of a more select, if seldom read, variety than that favored by the less-literary SVs, for the library tables of the former usually displayed elegantly bound sets of

Shakespeare (usually with uncut pages), occasionally supplemented by the more daring with slender volumes of the amorous poetical yearnings of Edna St. Vincent Millay or Sara Teasdale.

As a rule the gatherings of the Pierians went off smoothly with only a few snores to divert the attention of the more dedicated "culture vultures" from the lecturer or musical performer. But there was one time when an unscheduled divertissement by one of the members took the guest speaker, if not those who had gathered to hear him, by surprise.

On that never-to-be-forgotten afternoon the ladies had gathered to be enlightened by a prestigious tweedy Northern college professor wearing horn-rimmed glasses on the knottier problems of the poetry of Edwin Arlington Robinson. Everything went smoothly until the speaker identified Robinson with New England.

At that revelation, a little old lady in the front row leaped to her feet, pirouetted toward the audience and announced, "Girls, that reminds me, I've just returned from a delightful motor trip through New England during which I visited Portland, Maine, the birthplace of the immortal American poet, Henry Wordsworth (sic) Longfellow."

This disclosure was greeted with a mixed murmur of surprise and approbation, after which the woman continued, "Most of you will recall that I recited 'The Wreck of the Hesperus' when I graduated from Mary Custis Lee Female Seminary, and since I still remember every word of it, I'm going to recite it for you now."

Meanwhile, the speaker had removed his glasses and stood in stunned silence as the woman hopped up on the platform, assumed a heroic pose, and launched into the poem, punctuating each line with exaggerated dramatic and pathetic gestures. Finally, when she had gone through all twenty-two stanzas and wound up her recitation with a resounding:

Such was the wreck of the Hesperus
In the midnight and the snow!

Christ save us all from a death like this
On the reef of Norman's Woe!

she curtsied, jumped nimbly down from the dais, and resumed her seat amidst deafening applause.

By then the speaker was so intimidated, he had difficulty concentrating on what he had to impart. Later, when one of the flower-hatted Pierians offered him a cup of tea, he declined, mopped his brow with his handkerchief, then whispered, "You don't have anything *stronger*, do you?," adding "After that experience I really need it!"

Usually the Pierians were unanimous in their choice of speakers, but on one occasion one of the members, a highly-critical matron, demurred when it was proposed to invite a long-winded clergyman of whom she disapproved for a return engagement. Since she was outvoted, however, the woman said no more, but bided her time. On the day of the lecture she arrived early and took her usual place in a front row chair, referred to by one of the sharper-tongued Pierians as "the seat of the scornful."

After being welcomed by the club president, the speaker placed a hefty sheaf of notes on the lectern, adjusted his pince-nez, which he wore on a long black ribbon around his neck, and launched into a decidedly biased discourse on the benefits that Christianity had supposedly brought to the Virginia Indians. In the meantime, the disapproving woman stared at him so fixedly through her tortoise shell lorgnette he apparently decided to even old scores by embarrassing her publicly.

When he observed she had begun to squirm, he paused in mid-sentence, glowered down at her, and enquired loftily, "Pardon me, ma'am, is my talk making you restless?" "Certainly not," the woman replied with a wicked chuckle, "I'm following the Christian precept of turning the other cheek!"

On a later occasion the same woman was responsible for the discomforture of another of the club's speakers. That particular year the Pierians were deep in the study of Shakespeare. Unfortunately the regular lecturer had to cancel his appearance because of illness and his place was taken by an airy Queensport bluestocking who had offered to share her meditations on the Freudian symbolism in "Macbeth" with her sister members.

When the day of the lecture arrived, she mounted the platform wearing a large uptilted picture hat profusely decorated with green velvet leaves. At that point the stiletto-tongued Pierian nudged another member seated beside her and commented in a loud stage whisper, "Lord have mercy! Birnam Wood is moving to Dunsinane!"

That the sublime and the ridiculous are frequently interchangeable is also apparent from another Pierian Spring Club episode dating from the nineteen-twenties, the period of the flapper, the cake-eater and the hip flask - the perfect background for the sensational divorce proceedings between Edward West Browning, an aging New York Sybarite, then starring in the national headlines as "Daddy" Browning, and his blonde, teen-age bride, the former Frances Belle Heenan, whom her besotted spouse had earlier nicknamed "Peaches."

The details of this asinine story, which kicked off one of the most flamboyant binges of rococo prose in the history of American journalism, can easily be found in any comprehensive social history of the period. But they need not detain us, for it was one of the Pierians' reaction to the scandal, rather that the national one, that concerns us here.

Shortly after the Brownings' bedroom shenanigans had ceased to occupy front page billing in practically every newspaper in the country, the Pierians devoted an afternoon to discussing the literary output of the British poet, Robert Browning, during which generous excerpts from his works were read aloud. All went well until the chairman completed the reading of a particularly obscure poem, at which time one matron cleared her throat loudly and asked, "Did Browning really write that?"

"Why, yes," the reader replied.

"Well," the questioner snorted, "no wonder Peaches divorced him!"

As a rule the Pierians discouraged male attendance at their meetings, but once a year they sponsored a cultural binge to which reluctant husbands and other male members of their families were dragooned into attending a couple of hours of extra-special poetry and music. The entrapped victims usually survived by secretly taking along well-filled pocket flasks to share in the men's room before the program got under way. In any event, an incident which occurred at one of these affairs quickly became a part of Queensport's scatological history.

The night was hot and humid and every window in the auditorium was wide open to admit what little breeze was stirring. After things got under way, the poetical dronings, interspersed with violin and piano renditions of Massenet's "Elegy" and Dvorak's "Humoresque," began to be punctuated by the ominous rumblings of a rapidly approaching thunderstorm.

Undeterred, the sweating performers continued, and the final selection on the program, a spirited flute and piano accompanied rendition of "Lo, Hear the Gentle Lark" by an overweight, would-be Queensport coloratura, was almost over when a sudden flash of lighting shot through the auditorium. Its advent coincided with the singer's anticipated concluding E-flat in altisimo, but she never achieved it.

The flash unnerved her so completely she lost control and farted so loudly that one of the long-suffering, half-tipsy male victims in the audience cried out, "My God! She must be relieved!" Mercifully, a loud clap of thunder followed by a torrential downpour put a speedy termination to the occasion.

" . . . under a card-table canopy"

7. A Cloud-Cuckoo-Land Assortment

The South has long been noted for its eccentrics, but Queensport, as far as I have ever been able to discover, was the only Dixie community where a woman habitually slept with an improvised card table canopy over her head to prevent the cracked ceiling of her bedroom from falling in on her during the night. When the plaster finally gave way, with such a vengeance that the table was demolished and the woman had to be hospitalized, her friends were not so much solicitous for her injuries as peeved with a denouement that had deprived them of a cherished zany situation.

This picturesque manifestation was not unique, however, for there were dozens of other Queensport cases which caused it to be referred to in staider Virginia circles as "that Bedlam without bars." For instance, there was the blunt-spoken citizen of distinguished lineage who, scorning the use of window screens in any season, always shrouded his handsome family portraits (pronounced "pawtrets" in Queensport) in green cheesecloth during the summer months.

When asked to explain this unusual practice, he replied loftily, "I don't want the Goddamned plebeian flies defecating on the faces of my aristocratic forebears." Although scatologically reprehensible, his answer was nevertheless applauded in upper crust Queensport circles, being regarded as an ingenious manner of emphasizing the importance of ancestor worship, a cult assiduously practiced by his peers.

Then there was the eccentric Queensport spinster of beanpole proportions, known familiarly as Miss Alice, who had taken up her residence near the high school I attended long before I first crossed its threshold. Rumor reported a blow on the head when she was young had sent Miss Alice off her rocker. Others maintained that her Ophelia-like vagueness had been caused by having been jilted in her youth by an attractive cad for a more voluptuous damsel. Be that as it may, Miss Alice's zany aberrations were a delightful relief from the routine of Queensport's everyday existence, and by the time I got to know her she was affectionately regarded as one of the town's most interesting characters.

Standing six feet in her French-heeled, high-buttoned shoes, Miss Alice always wore a big flower-decorated hat atop her disorderly coiffeur, a pair of pince-nez perched on the bridge of her aquiline nose, and a long duster-like coat reaching to her ankles fastened down its buttonless front with big brass horse-blanket safety pins. Her only other adornment was a small Confederate battle flag on a gilded wooden staff which she held rigidly upright in her right hand at all times.

As someone decidedly out of the ordinary, Miss Alice was a great favorite with the boys and girls, most of whom, I am happy to recall, treated her with great deference. What is more, if she could be persuaded to recite her favorite poem beginning, "O, young Lochinvar is come out of the west," accompanied with sighs, fluttering eyelids and airy gesticulations, they were in the seventh heaven of delight.

Even so, Miss Alice's big moment had nothing to do with her recitation of Sir Walter Scott's poetical warhorse. The climax of her eccentric career came one early summer day when I was a sophomore and was so memorable it automatically elevated her to a permanent place in Queensport's already rich folklore.

It was "big recess" time and we were waiting for the clanging bell to call us back to classes when a man ran up yelling, "A naked woman just bust loose a few blocks down the street from here!" That was all we needed, and in no time everyone in the schoolyard had joined the posse of panting policemen and civilians who were in hot pursuit of a tall, clothesless woman who was dashing ahead of them. One look was all we needed to realize it was Miss Alice minus her usual long coat, but she was still wearing her floppy hat and high-heeled shoes and holding her small Confederate flag on high as she lured her pursuers onward.

Then the unexpected happened, for instead of continuing in a straight line, Miss Alice veered suddenly into a side street leading to Queensport's oldest and most prestigious cemetery, where the chase finally ended in a lot where a life-sized white marble, heaven-pointing angel gazed impersonally down on the commotion. By then we had learned that Miss Alice had been sitting quietly all morning under an umbrella tree in a nearby park when she suddenly shed her coat, revealing she was wearing nothing underneath. Immediately afterward, she had taken off.

The situation was touchy to say the least, as Miss Alice had abandoned her coat at the scene of her departure, but a cemetery maintenance man finally arose to the occasion and flung her a large artificial grass mat, the kind used around graves at funerals. Wrapping this around herself like an imperial emerald-tinted toga, Miss Alice lifted her tiny banner above her head like an oriflamme, called out "The Confederacy Forever!", and strode majestically toward the cemetery entrance.

Later, when she was asked by the desk sergeant at the police station why she had staged her impromptu return to nature, Miss Alice regarded him condescendingly for a moment, adjusted her pince-nez, and then answered archly, "I was feeling a trifle warm!"

There was also the superannuated Queensport dowager of my childhood who was satirically referred to as Zo Zo the Tinsel Queen because of her fondness for appearing in circus parades. Ordinarily this woman remained in bed all day reading highly romantic novels, only bestirring herself around dusk to arise and don a wig (she had one for every day in the week) and hastily dress for dinner. After that, she played whist with three equally ancient crones until the arrival of the milkman reminded her it was time to turn off the gas chandelier over the card table and go to bed again.

This year-in-and-year-out routine was changed only when a circus arrived in town, at which time the dowager would ring for Melodius Melody, her ancient black retainer, who had received his unique name because his mother had heard an organ grinder performing in the neighborhood when he was born. When he arrived at the dowager's bedside, she would give him a couple of dollars and send him to a confectionery to blow it all on penny suckers.

After that he would hitch up the dowager's dilapidated victoria, and when the circus parade got under way, he and his mistress would take up a position behind the steam calliope that ended the procession. But that didn't mean that they were lost in the shuffle, for the dowager always managed to upstage all that had gone before her by lavishly dispensing the suckers to the urchins who crowded around her carriage, delighted to be the recipients of her largess.

By and large, however, Queensport's prize aristocratic eccentrics were the identical twin sisters who were usually referred to as Nod and Bob because their constant head-shakings were the only way most people could tell them apart. Fortunately, one nodded her head over her right shoulder, while the other bobbed hers over her left, thereby considerably simplifying the process of identification. Fiercely conservative, both women strenuously resisted any modernizing of the neighborhood which their red brick, Richardson Romanesque house dominated, and their intransigence managed to fend off any twentieth century improvements until their deaths.

To be more specific, on one occasion the Queensport Electric Company sent one of its crews to install a street light in front of their house. Catching sight of the workmen digging a hole prior to putting up the light pole, the more aggressive sister stalked out of the house and demanded what they were doing. When she learned the reason for the excavation, of which she disapproved on general principles, she summoned her sister, after which the two of them got down in the hole. When the foreman protested, the women ignored him. Finally, the exasperated man telephoned his supervisor, who happened to be a cousin of the two women, and asked him what to do.

There was a slight pause, after which the supervisor asked, "They wouldn't by any chance be the _____ sisters, would they?" When his query was answered in the affirmative, the supervisor replied, "Help 'em out of the damned hole, fill it up, then see that they get back in the house safely! After that, report back here for another assignment!"

The deceased only brother of these characters had been a great admirer of the mystery stories of S. S. Van Dyne, and this made such an impression on them that they saw to it that even death did not deprive him of his pleasure. The way they did it would have been a deep and dark secret, however, if a Queensport bookseller hadn't leaked the information that when a new Van Dyne mystery came out, they not only bought a copy, but took it out to the cemetery and read it out loud to their departed brother.

The same brother had also collected string from the time he was a boy. By the time he died, his hoard, carefully squirrelled away in discarded shoe boxes, filled a small attic room from floor to ceiling. Before the sisters "passed on" several years later, a torrential rainstorm penetrated the slate roof of their home, doing considerable damage to the collection.

But that didn't faze the guardians of the string sanctuary. According to widely circulated gossip, one of the sisters told a neighbor, "After the roof was repaired, we had the servants hang out Brother's string collection on the clotheslines in the sun, and when it was dry, we packed it all up in new boxes in fresh tissue paper and stored it in the attic again."

8. Christianity With Rococo Trimmings

If I had not been gifted with a good boy-soprano voice, I might have remained a Hard-shell Baptist until I arrived at the age of reason and began to use my head for more than a hat-rack. My ability to carry a tune around a corner in a basket without dropping it altered the situation. When the snootiest Episcopal church in Queensport advertised for boy choristers shortly after my family moved there, I applied, was auditioned and accepted, and wound up a juvenile wage-earner in less time that it takes a miser to fish for change for a nickel out of a collection plate.

I couldn't have picked a better diamond horseshoe seat for my observation and eventual indoctrination into arcane Episcopal practices, for the church that paid for my piping soprano efforts was the most prestigious and snobbish temple of the Lord in Queensport. Even so, the congregation, like the Holy Trinity, was of a triune nature, a divisive situation which guaranteed constant ecclesiastical warfare without benefit of even an occasional truce.

To be more explicit, there was the Anglo-Catholic element which did all it could to emulate the ritualistic shenanigans legitimately practiced at a Roman Catholic establishment a few blocks away. Then there were the Low Church families, made up principally of the conservative old Queensport gentry, who were sneeringly refer-

" . . . the resounding blast was so loud and long . . . "

red to by the holier-than-thou Anglo-Catholics as the "hat-in-the-font-and-umbrella-on-the-altar crowd."

In between were the run-of-the-mill Protestant Episcopalians consisting largely of social climbers who had moved up from the lowlier evangelical ranks to assure that their daughters might qualify to make their debuts at the Queensport Cotillion Club and be joined later in holy matrimony to some impecunious scion of the Old Guard in the proper ecclesiastical setting.

The arena for these so-called Christian goings-on was a handsome structure. As the rectors who arbitrated the sacerdotal gladiatorial contests carried on there were all clerical egoists, everything possible in the way of theatrical ritual, highlighted with rich vestments, flaming candles, bejewelled crosses, soul-inspiring music and spectacular pageantry, was encouraged to provide a solemnly meretricious experience. Having been reared until then on the dry husks of spartan Southern Baptist piety, I found the effect overwhelming, and it was not long before I had joined the Anglo-Catholic contingent and was priggishly genuflecting and crossing myself with the best of them.

The aftereffect of an unintentional accident which took place at my confirmation, however, might have had something to do with this heady change. On the day the bishop was present for the ceremonial laying on of hands, I stole from my place in the choir to the altar rail to await his ministrations. I got them, too, with a vengeance! When the time came for him to lay his hands on my head and begin the familiar "Defend, O Lord, this Thy Child" rigmarole, his heavy gold episcopal ring reversed on his thin old finger, and when his hands came down on my head, my skull got the full impact of its massive setting in a resounding crack that echoed throughout the sanctuary.

In sober retrospect, I must admit the churchly window-trimmings I have been describing meant very little to me in the long run, for in looking back the amusing things that happened at that time far outnumber those of a more solemn and lastingly serious nature. For instance, I shall never forget an episode which took place one Easter Sunday that almost resulted in all of the boy choristers being packed off to the juvenile lockup.

The church sanctuary on that never-to-be-forgotten morning was banked with lilies, while dozens of tall wax tapers provided the proper operatic setting for Gounod's "St. Cecilia Mass," the prime example of eau de cologne musical piety featured that Sunday. Everyone, with the exception of the dyed-in-the-wool low churchmen in the congregation, had been uplifted to the proper pitch of Resurrection devotion when an accident suddenly shattered the solemnity of the occasion.

The principal acolyte that morning was a small boy whose influential socialite mother had pressured the reluctant rector into allowing him to serve on the altar for the festive celebration. Decked out in a scarlet cassock and white, lace-trimmed cotta, the pint-sized functionary went through his paces perfectly until the time came to take up the offering.

It was a feast day and the collection was proportionately large. As the ushers in striped trousers, cutaway coats, bat-wing collars and ascot ties stacked the overflowing silver plates into the huge alms basin held out unsteadily by the boy, it immediately dawned on every chorister looking on that he would never make it to the high altar without a mishap. A flourish of organ trumpets diverted us momentarily, however, and we turned to the altar to chant, "All things come of Thee O Lord, and of Thine own have we given Thee."

The same wheeling movement was also attempted by the acolyte with his precariously balanced burden. Suddenly there was a resounding crash of silver alms basins, while greenbacks, coins and church envelopes flew in all directions. Even so, the minuscule server doggedly bore what was left to the altar for the customary blessing. Since there was no possible way the spilled offering could be retrieved until after the service, we could hardly sing for looking at the tempting loot flung so advantageously in our path.

When the recessional finally got under way it was a case of "Let not thy right hand know what thy left is doing." Balancing his hymnal on one hand, each choirboy did a little private retrieving on his own as he filed out of the chancel, but the ill-gotten booty was not long in returning where it belonged. Our choir director, having taken in the situation from the organ bench, locked all of us in the practice room, secured the strong-arm assistance of the adult male singers, and shook us down to the tune of more than two hundred dollars before we were permitted to go home and eat our Easter Sunday dinners.

On another occasion when I had the lead soprano solo part in the "Inflammatus" from Rossini's "Stabat Mater", I ruined the performance by my lack of attention. The fault was more or less excusable, however, for on that particular Sunday a harmless, socially prominent eccentric, whose habit while attending church was to toss salted peanuts into the air and catch them in his mouth, had turned up for the special music.

All went well, however, until we began the florid Rossini number which I was to lead off over a pulsating agitato accompaniment on the organ. At that moment I looked down into the congregation from the choir stalls and saw the Peanut Eater, as we called him, putting on his act, much to the annoyance of the worshipers around him. The sight was so fascinating I completely missed my cue, the result being my pay was docked for the rest of the month.

Strangely enough, I can hardly remember any of the whited sepulchers who served as rectors of the church while I was a boy soprano, but my memories of the Low Church bishop who confirmed me are still vivid. As his churchmanship was spartan by comparison with the ritualistic grand opera performed where I was a chorister, he limited his visits to one Sunday in the year, the day set apart for the rite of confirmation.

One of these occasions, apart from the time I got knocked on the head with his ecclesiastical ring, stands out vividly in my memory because of a prank played on the old fellow by one of the choirboys whose voice was the only angelic thing about him.

That Sunday, the chorister in question turned up with a big rubber doughnut-shaped whoopee cushion in a cardboard box. When no one was looking, he sneaked into the church before the service, inflated it and secreted it under the blue velvet cushion in the seat of the bishop's throne in the sanctuary. Since no one knew what he had done, the surprise, when it came, was catastrophic.

After we had filed up the aisle singing, "Rise, crowned with light, Imperial Salem rise!," accompanied by fanfares on the organ, there was a brief pause, after which the bishop turned to the congregation, held up his hands, and called out in a quavering voice, "The Lord is in His holy temple: let all the earth keep silence before Him." Then the regular clergyman made preparations to read the opening prayers of the service.

In the split second between the bishop's invocation and the priest's intention, however, the former sat down heavily on his throne and the resounding blast that resulted from the pressure of his ample buttocks on the booby trap planted beneath the blue velvet cushion was so loud and long the rest of the service was an antiphonal combination of hilarity and ill-attempted music making.

9. Latter-Day Usurpers of Adam's Role

Adam might have been the first gardener, but his Queensport female descendants during my salad days were among the most dedicated latter-day usurpers of his divinely appointed role. Inspired by a mild climate, good soil, and a militant rivalry to snare the top prizes at any flower show, however inconsequential, the town's lady gardeners entered the horticultural lists like so many self-appointed crusaders armed with trowels and watering cans.

If the artificial flowers on their dress parade hats were more resplendent and enduring than the ones they grew, it was not because they had neglected the age-old urge to accomplish the perfect union of seeds, cuttings and a well-rotted compost pile. Nursery catalogs and gardening manuals vied in popularity with the light love stories of Gene Stratton Porter as the favorite reading matter of the greater part of the female sector of Queensport's gardeners. Also, any lecturer, even if he hailed from north of the Mason and Dixon Line, who could demonstrate how to grow anything bigger and better from azaleas to zinnias was regarded by the floral faithful as a prophet definitely with honor, in or out of his own country.

The discovery of a new variety of flower or shrub had the same effect on Queensport's lady horticulturists as the first taste of liquor has on an alcoholic, while the possession of a "green thumb" (i.e., the ability to grow anything, no matter how reluctant) was regarded in the same category as having a Confederate general as a grand-

"Attached to the rope was a crudely lettered sign. . ."

father. Those possessing the gift were looked upon by the less fortunate as specially anointed pulpiteers of the floral apostolic succession.

As one Queensport matron so gifted once expressed it to a Doubting Thomas who had brought an ailing geranium to her for the laying on of hands, "Why, I could even stick *you* in the ground and wind up making you blossom like Aaron's rod!"

Of course, frantic gardening activity of that intensity was bound to throw off a few humorous sparks. For instance, there was the tale of the two ardent Queensport flower lovers who visited the ruined ancestral home of one of the principals, a place once famous for its high living, particularly of the alcoholic kind. While poking through the weed-choked grounds, the visitors discovered a neglected rose bush, a variety formerly known throughout Virginia by the name of the family who originally owned the estate. Each visitor took home a cutting and planted it.

A year or so later the descendent of the Colonial hell-raisers was entertaining the other woman at a dinner party. In the center of the table was a large porcelain bowl filled with delicately tinted pink roses. When the guest admired them extravagantly and asked where they came from, the hostess told her they were blossoms from the rooted cutting of the rose bush she had brought home from her ancestral bailiwick.

"You do have all the luck," the other woman sighed. "Why, I planted my cutting and tended it like a baby but it died."

"How did you cultivate it?" the hostess asked.

"Why, I watered it, of course," the other woman replied.

"Lord have mercy, no wonder it croaked," the hostess commented dryly. "You should have had better sense than to attempt to nurture anything bearing my family name with anything as innocuous as water!"

Queensport's annual Garden Week was the high spot on its floral calendar, and on one of those occasions a mixup occurred in a special supplement to the *Courier*, the town's morning paper, which turned out to be the equivalent of palming off stinkweed for sweet peas. The front page of the section was illustrated with two six-column pictures. One depicted a grim collection of flower-hatted female battle axes who had recently been elected as officers of the Queensport Cape Jasmine Society. The other cut showed the ruins of a nearby pre-Revolutionary church.

Somehow the cuts got transposed, and when the public got around to reading the lines under the picture of the women, they were jolted with the following: "These venerable Virginia ruins will be thrown open to the public for the first time this year during Queensport Garden Week."

As a rule those who owned handsome or historic houses were asked to open them for a fee during the annual floral saturnalia, and this custom was responsible for two of Queensport's choicest yarns. The first concerned how a bellicose ancient spinster won her point when she was coerced into exhibiting the home in which she had resided all of her life.

The house was jointly owned by the spinster, her widowed sister, and the widow's son. The spinster was adamant in her refusal to permit the ragtag and bobtail of Queensport to violate her privacy, but she was eventually outvoted by the two other members of her family. Under pressure she was forced to give in, but in doing so she won a memorable triumph.

When the day for displaying the house arrived, those who paid to walk over its threshold encountered an unexpected hilarious treat. The spinster, brandishing a baseball bat, had ensconced herself on a stool in one corner of the parlor. Before her stretched a heavy rope, one end of which was anchored to an andiron, the other to the carved cabriole leg of a square grand piano. Attached to the rope was a crudely lettered sign. It read: "THIS IS MY THIRD, GOD DAMN IT! KEEP OUT!"

The other Garden Week incident involved a memorable locking of horns between a Queensport grande dame who lived in one of the town's few architecturally distinctive old houses and a brash male member of the nouveaux riches. Usually when the matron permitted the general public to poke and pry among her ancestral treasures, she retired above-stairs and turned over the lower floor to the official hostesses, but the year the incident occurred she was forced by circumstances to alter her procedure.

After the Johnny-come-lately arrived in his chauffeur-driven limousine and had paid his entrance fee, he brushed off the suggestion that an official hostess show him around, demanding instead to speak with the lady of the house. When the latter reluctantly joined him in the lower hall, a few preliminaries were quickly dispensed with. Then the paying guest got down to brass tacks.

He was thinking of building a mansion, he volunteered, and had instructed his architect to copy the doorway of the matron's home down to the smallest detail. After she had complimented him on his good taste, he added that the new doorway would not be complete unless it included a replica of the handsome brass knocker that adorned the entrance to the old home.

He then announced his intention of borrowing the knocker in order that an exact copy could be make of it. That suggestion was countered by the matron who protested that the knocker had never been off the door since the house was built. Even so, the determined bounder swept that technicality aside as a mere bagatelle.

"Oh, that won't be any problem at all," he said with a wink. "I investigated the situation before you came downstairs, and I discovered the knocker is only fastened to the door with two screws."

Confronted with such brashness, the matron drew herself up to her full height, and then let the boor have it with both barrels. "I know," she said archly, "but you failed to take in a *very* important detail when you were conducting your investigation - the screws are on *my* side of the door!"

10. They Also Served

No collection of Queensport anecdotes would be complete without including a few outstanding gems concerning the faithful black retainers who patiently endured the vagaries of the town's upper crust, many of whom were closely related to their servitors on the wrong side of the blanket.

To illustrate the point, on one occasion when a Queensport matron advertised for a laundress, a handsome black woman whom the matron's brother was known to be keeping as his paramour applied for the job. Accompanying her were several children, ranging in color from black to mulatto.

When the matron asked if all of the children belonged to the prospective employee, she was told in no uncertain terms that they did. After a moment, the matron remarked that the children were of different colors. To this, their mother replied, "Dat's right, ma'am, but see hits lak dis. My fust husban' was black lak me an' my secon' one was brown; but de nice gent'man I'se now keepin' company wid belongs to de fair sex."

Although not as sociologically significant as that tale, there is another yarn concerning a former Queensporter who was famous as a raconteur. As a result he was not only a welcome guest wherever his friends gathered to enjoy good wining and dining enlivened by witty story-telling, he was equally popular at his own table.

Once when he was regaling a large dinner party in his home with a particularly funny story, he was interrupted by the dignified old black man who had served as his butler for years. Entering the dining room on tiptoe, the

"*She's sufferin' from nervous prostitution . . .*"

butler bent over his employer and whispered audibly, "Suh, how 'bout entertainin' dese folks heah wid anuthuh long-winded yarn. De secon' co'se won't be ready fo anuthuh tin minits."

Then there is this time-honored Queensport story concerning an Episcopal clergyman who arrived in the city to officiate at a special Sunday evening service only to find that his absentminded wife had packed a soiled surplice instead of a clean one in his traveling bag. When this was discovered, his thoughtful hostess took over and handed the grimy vestment to her laundress, after which she joined her family and her guest at dinner.

A few moments later, the fried chicken, Smithfield ham and batter bread routine was interrupted by the laundress who peered cautiously around the door leading from the kitchen. When the hostess looked in her direction, the laundress inquired in a loud stage whisper, "Missus, does de archangel want his shimmy sta'ched or plain?"

On another occasion around the turn of the century the flighty wife of a Queensport doctor paid a formal call on a new bride who had recently returned from her honeymoon. Greeted at the front door by the parlor maid, she placed her calling card on a silver salver in the hall and asked the maid to announce her presence to her mistress, who was above-stairs.

The newlywed was famous for her sharp tongue and the fact that she didn't suffer fools readily. When the maid told her who was downstairs, she let her feelings be known in no uncertain terms. "Oh, that bore," she remarked in a voice that was easily heard in the parlor below. "Tell her I can't come down. Say I'm suffering from nervous prostration." After descending the stairs, the maid poked her head around the parlor door and delivered a slightly different version of the message. "Honey," she said, "Missus can't come down. She's sufferin' from nervous prostitution."

There is also this gem concerning an elderly black Queensport cook and a visiting New England matron.

The culinary efforts of the cook were celebrated for their tastiness, but the kitchen over which she presided was so lacking in cleanliness that those in the know rarely partook of her delicacies.

On one occasion, however, her employer, who cared little concerning the condition of her kitchen so long as the food got on the table, was entertaining a group of visiting members of a national patriotic organization at a high noon breakfast. The New England matron was among the guests and was impressed with the dainty beaten biscuits the cook had prepared. Having never seen, much less tasted, a beaten biscuit, she asked her hostess for the recipe, only to be told airily that she never entered her kitchen, but would be happy to call the cook and get the recipe for her.

When the cook was summoned and asked for the recipe, she dictated it in a rambling and incoherent manner. The Yankee matron then proceeded to praise the pricked decorations on the tops of the biscuits and asked how they were accomplished, only to be floored by the answer.

Taking a battered white celluloid comb from her hair, the cook put the finishing touch on her recipe. "Well, honey, hit's dis way," she said. "Ah has dis heah ol' comb in my hair, and when Ah gits ready to poke dem biskits in de oben, Ah jest takes it out an' gew-gaws 'em up a bit."

11. Cultural Citadel With a Difference

When Andrew Carnegie's munificence made the first Queensport public library possible around the turn of the century he little realized what a mare's nest of quirkiness his generosity engendered. Everything about the place from its theatrical but impractical marble staircase to the fly-specked plaster bust of Jefferson Davis in the reading room, frequently used as a hat-rack by an irreverent board member, smacked of genteel eccentricity.

As for the staff, from the head librarian, a barely breathing replica of the granite effigy of Pallas that presided over the main portal, down to the sybaritic old janitor whose rheumy eyes were always cocked in the direction of any attractive young male patron, it was in perfect keeping with the offbeat character of the establishment.

In those days, professional library training was not regarded as important in Queensport. If you were a woman, belonged to an old family and were sufficiently cantankerous, you automatically qualified as a dispenser of publicly-owned books. To cross one of these crotchety viragos could be a perilous experience, but if you had the good sense to stay in the background and keep a sharp lookout, the everyday workings of the Queensport library were a liberal education in human perversity.

To illustrate the point, one irate patron became so incensed at the curt way he was treated by the unrecon-

"... taking his siesta ..."

structed vestals who staffed the reference room when the library was first opened he retaliated by scribbling this quatrain on one of the outside columns of the building:

> The bust of Pallas frowning o'er the door
> Of the new library is proudly prim;
> But watch your step - the dames who work inside
> Are much more haughty, acid-tongued and grim!

To insert a personal memory, I vividly recall the ancient spinster who drilled me with a pair of steely Confederate-gray eyes when I first applied for library membership and demanded "What side of the war (she said "de Wah") did your folks fight on?" When I informed her that my maternal grandfather had been one of Grant's boys in a Union suit, she immediately subjected me to a verbal barrage that put the bombardment of Fort Sumter in the shade.

In keeping with the gossipy character of the establishment, the entire staff knocked off every afternoon at four o'clock to descend the marble staircase to a first-floor hideaway (genteelly referred to by those who affected the broad-A as the "Stahf Room") to exchange scandalous tidbits over tea and cookies. At those times a shelver was left in charge of the circulation desk and the regular business of the library was halted until the tea and rumor factory closed down. This arrangement was a daily ritual for years until an unexpected interruption revealed that other things beside gossip were the order of the day during these sessions.

At that time, all books of a questionable nature were kept under lock and key in the head librarian's office, and were issued only to those whose moral armament, in her opinion, was sufficiently impregnable to withstand the blandishments of sexual titillation. The year of the incident, Edmund Wilson's "Memoirs of Hecate County" had burst like a stink bomb on the national literary scene and it was only after much debate that it was added to the library's collection.

Even so, the book was not accessible to the general public, while it was automatically taken for granted by the board members that the librarians were too pure in mind to even dream of peering between its covers. Word got around, however, that the forbidden fictional fruit was available to a favored few, and one of the city's more liberal minded young women asked for permission to read it. As she belonged to a socially prominent family, she could hardly be denied the privilege. She was therefore notified that the book would be reserved for her at the checkout desk in a sealed brown paper envelope bearing her name if she would call for it in person.

Her visit to the library coincided with the afternoon staff tea party, and the shelver left in charge was unable to find the package. This so enraged the patron, who was notorious for her short temper, that she rushed down the stairs to confront the gossipers to learn why the book had not been reserved for her as promised.

When she flung open the door of the scandal sanctuary, however, she was stopped in her tracks. Instead of finding a chitchat session in full swing, she discovered a bevy of breathless, open-mouthed spinsters perched on the edges of their chairs listening to a particularly salacious portion of the book being read aloud by another librarian.

The official reaction to the revelation that the staff had been surreptitiously sampling the more lubricous items in the collection brought on an about-face puritanical policy that resulted in placing even "Gray's Anatomy" on the Queensport index expurgatorius. From then on if a patron desired to consult that or any other restricted book, he was chaperoned by a latter-day staff disciple of Anthony Comstock, who sat beside him in the reading room to guarantee he was not flipping through the pages for prurient purposes.

Apart from magazines and newspapers, the library reading room contained little more at that time than a couple of sets of outdated encyclopedias, dog-eared dictionaries, the multi-volume records of the Southern Confederacy, genealogical quarterlies, and well-thumbed copies of "Burke's Peerage" and the same author's "Landed Gentry." The latter volumes were always reserved each Wednesday for a couple of maiden ladies who augmented their income by climbing family trees and painting coats of arms, authentic or otherwise, for those desiring to connect themselves with the illustrious of the past.

With clock-like regularity on their appointed day for research, these old biddies would descend on the library in a venerable electric brougham that moved through the hectic downtown traffic with the self-conscious dignity of a whale among darting minnows. One of them brought along pencils, drawing pads, watercolors, notebooks, assorted brushes and a large magnifying glass, while the other lugged Thomas Jefferson, their big yellow tomcat, under one arm, and a shallow wooden box and a paper bag of sand under the other.

Before settling down for a session with Burke and the genealogical quarterlies, the sisters would concoct a temporary comfort station with the box and sand for their cat's use in the library stacks, after which they concentrated on digging up ancestors for their gullible clients. Their findings were rarely correct, however, for there was the story of a socially ambitious family that displayed one of their heraldic confections for years, believing it was the authentic blazoning of their family coat of arms, only to learn later that its origin was highly questionable.

The brave dream of once-possessed dukedoms of that particular clan was shot down by a sharp-eyed Yankee acquaintance, who pointed out that the motto "Ex Libris" embellished on a scroll beneath the shield proved conclusively that the armorial bearings they had paid for were more fanciful than correct.

While the perpetrators of this fraudulent emblazonment were busy with their pads and paint brushes, their cat had the run of the library, and was frequently observed by the patrons taking his siesta draped around the dirty plaster bust of Jefferson Davis in the reading room. Later, when his owners had finished their diggings for the day and had settled on copying "the prettiest in the lot" when they encountered several coats of arms for unrelated families of the same name, they would empty their kitty's temporary loo, gather up their questionable genealogical gleanings, and head for home in their ancient electric car.

Like all libraries, the Queensport book depository was constantly plagued with persons who insisted on keeping out books overtime, a deplorable habit which resulted in at least one memorable fracas. The principal was a testy sexpot who had been pestered for weeks to return a copy of "Forever Amber" which she had checked out months earlier. Finally, when all hope of retrieving the book had been abandoned, the woman stormed up the marble stairs of the library and demanded to speak with the head librarian.

When she appeared, the angry woman insisted on knowing why she had been repeatedly annoyed by overdue notices, asserting that she had never checked out the book they were hounding her to return. As the argument waxed hotter, the complainer finally felt the urge to throw something. Reaching into her shopping bag, she pulled out a hefty volume, hurled it at the librarian's head, and then swept angrily down the stairs.

After the screen door at the entrance had loudly proclaimed her departure, the startled librarian picked up the literary missile. It was the overdue book. But that wasn't the end of the story. When the volume was checked in, it was discovered that the patron had been using a condom as a bookmark!

There was also another hilarious incident which caused a good deal of embarrassment to the head librarian who was conducting a group of out-of-town dignitaries over the facility when it occurred. All of the staff members had been warned to be on their best behavior during the visitation, but the best laid plans of the library chief were shattered when a very determined and eccentric dowager who was unaware of what was in progress stalked through the main portal.

The woman suffered from arthritis which prevented her from climbing the marble stairs leading to the main desk. Catching the eye of one of the staffers on duty there, she imperiously signaled that she send down a shelver immediately to pick up the books she had just returned in a string bag. One of these was a recent biography of Nell Gwyn, which the dowager had enjoyed so thoroughly that she apparently wanted to continue her investigation of the demimondaines of history.

Spotting the librarian who usually helped her with her book selection and completely disregarding the solemnity that was being observed for the distinguished visitors, she cupped her hands to her mouth like a megaphone and hallooed: "Got any more good books up there on whores?"

The best Queensport library yarn, however, is one in which I was peripherally involved. One day while browsing through the periodicals in the reading room I came across an esoteric literary quarterly called "Hound and Horn." Devoted exclusively to Henry James, that particular issue contained photographs of the novelist from the time he was a wide-eyed boy in a brass-buttoned pre-Civil War jacket to pictures of him in later life. As one of my friends was then reading James's novels, I recommended that she look it over.

Hastening to the library, she asked for the quarterly. When it could not be found in the reading room, she waited patiently while the ancient librarian on duty rummaged for it in the dusty stacks. Finally after some time had passed, the librarian emerged clutching a battered magazine in her hand. Shoving it across the counter to my friend, she croaked, "Hound and Horn ain't in, so I brought you the nearest thing we've got to it." Glancing at what was offered, my friend raised an amused eyebrow. It was a two-year-old copy of "Field and Stream."

" . . . a perky, beady-eyed mynah bird . . . "

12. Feathered and Furry Screwballs

Queensport had more than its quota of offbeat feathered and furry screwballs to augment the shenanigans of its two-legged characters. For instance, there was this episode which occurred before the advent of Prohibition.

At that time a timid schoolteacher boarded with one of the town's most militant widows who lived near the business area. In order to reach her school and return home the teacher had to walk by a popular saloon. As she was sadly lacking in any of the sexier attractions, however, she passed and repassed the place hundreds of times without being noticed by any of the womanizers who usually lolled outside its door.

Then one balmy spring afternoon as she was on her way home from school she was stopped in her tracks by a wolf whistle from a vine-shaded porch above the saloon. Before she could collect her wits a raucous male voice from behind the vines invited her upstairs for an uninhibited romp in the hay.

Fleeing in terror, the teacher reached her boarding house in a state of hysteria. She had hardly blurted out what had happened, however, before the boardinghouse keeper had put on her hat and was dragging her back to the scene of the incident, collecting an angry posse of belligerent female sympathizers on the way.

Bursting through the swinging doors of the saloon, the self-righteous mob put on a pretty good reenactment of the Assyrians coming down like wolves on the fold, while the bartender was so shocked by the sudden female invasion of his strictly all-male preserve he later declared he finally realized how Custer must have felt at Little Big Horn.

"It's a sorry how-de-do when an innocent woman can't walk by your den of iniquity without being grossly insulted," the boardinghouse keeper opened fire.

When the bartender registered surprise, the woman, acting as the schoolteacher's mouthpiece, recounted the episode in detail, omitting only the suggestive word used by the unidentified proposer of amorous dalliance. After she had finished, the bartender grinned. Then he commented, "Oh, is that what happened?" Walking from behind the bar he added, "Well, if you ladies will just follow me I'll be more than happy to introduce you to the culprit."

The schoolteacher and the champions of virtue trooped upstairs behind the bartender to his living quarters. When they reached the shady porch from which the whistle and invitation for an uninhibited romp had emanated earlier, he pointed to an upended box on which rested a large cage containing a perky, beady-eyed mynah bird. Before he could say anything, the bird gave the boardinghouse keeper a roguish wink, let out another shrill whistle, and screamed, "Let's screw, baby! Let's screw!"

"Well, ladies," the bartender said after the shocked tittering had subsided, "much as I hate to give up my pet, I suppose I'll have to do it before you ride me out of Queensport on a rail!"

The next avian anecdote linked Queensport's last deluxe horse-drawn funeral with some saucy parrot patter that was hardly appropriate for the occasion. One of the town's leading citizens died and as he was a great "jiner," belonging to every fraternal order in the city from the Elks to the Masons, everyone anticipated an extra special funeral.

The undertaker didn't disappoint them either, for in anticipation of the event his stable boys polished his ebony-enameled hacks and curried his high-stepping black horses until they gleamed. Since the deceased had been a state officer in the Knights Templar, his fellow members turned out in force - arrayed in splendid ceremonial gold-buttoned uniforms, swords, sashes and elegant white plumed hats - to do him honor.

The day of the funeral every front porch railing along the line of march to the cemetery was crowded with spectators, and on one of these verandas a big green parrot was present among those who eagerly anticipated the event. The parrot was a famous mimic, but until that day no one realized it had been paying close attention to the neighborhood boys as they yelled at one another while playing Cops and Robbers.

Everything went well until the Knights Templar strutted into view, proceeded by a snare drum corps beating out a solemn, muffled tread. Then, seemingly out of the blue, the parrot took over, shattering the solemnity of the occasion by squawking, "Head off the sons of bitches! Head 'em off!," following this outburst with a strident blast of mocking laughter. At that point, the parrot's owner rushed it into the house, but the damage had been done, for the Knights Templar were visibly shaken.

Shifting from Queensport's avian tradition to its feline lore, there was this tale concerning an agitated matron who telephoned a veterinarian and implored him to come to her house immediately to check on her listless female cat. The veterinarian came, examined the kitty, then reported it was in the family way.

"That can't be true!" the matron wailed. "I never take Puss in Boots out of the house unless I put her on a leash."

Just then another big black cat slunk from under the sofa on which the matron and the veterinarian were seated and began to strut self-consciously about the room. Observing that the animal was well-endowed testicle-wise, the veterinarian raised a knowing eyebrow and enquired, "What about him?"

"Oh, don't be silly," the matron exclaimed, "that's Pussy's brother Tom!," adding, "He wouldn't dream of getting intimate with his sister!"

To insert a personal anecdote, I well remember a post-Depression conversation that I had with a witty maiden lady who had lived all her life in one of Queensport's more notable old houses. In recalling the trying times that we, among countless others, had experienced during the Great Depression, I asked her banteringly if the wolf had ever knocked on her door during that time.

Her reply was classic. Fixing me with a amused eye, she quipped, "The particular wolf that knocked on *my* door was a female of the species, and she was so ungrateful she had quintuplets in my front hall the moment after I let her in."

Then there was Queenie! A fierce, spayed German police bitch with a penchant for mistaking the legs of anyone conveniently nearby for a fire plug, Queenie was the pride and joy of an indulgent elderly spinster who made it plain that she preferred the companionship of her undisciplined dog to that of her neighbors.

As a result, Queenie, who was never corrected in any way, was not only the terror of all mail carriers and delivery-men, she invariably used the choicest flower beds of dedicated gardeners within a wide radius as repositories for the bones she collected on her daily rounds.

A meal with Queenie's mistress was a wide-awake nightmare. Not only did her pet roam the dining room whining to be fed the choicest tidbits from the table, she greeted anyone reluctant to comply with such ferocious growls that any refuser usually wound up with a bad case of indigestion.

Queenie's insatiable craving for sweets also resulted in her being on intimate terms with the contents of the open sugar barrel in her mistress's pantry. If anyone remarked on the frosted condition of her facial hairs after one of these incursions, the observation was inevitably countered by her owner with, "Oh, didn't you know? Queenie has a sweet tooth!"

Queenie cut a wide swath through her particular bailiwick until her untimely death in a dog fight. After that, her distraught mistress reportedly had her pelt tanned and used it as a hearthrug in her boudoir. Before that turn of events, however, Queenie climaxed her belligerent career by making a spectacular raid on a nearby chicken yard, resulting in the demise of twenty or more prized Rhode Island Red hens.

Queenie's mistress had to pay for the damage, but she recouped her losses by surreptitiously using the victims of her pet's foray to concoct an abundant supply of chicken salad. This was served as the *piece de resistance* of an elaborate buffet, during which unsuspecting guests came back for second and third helpings, little realizing Queenie's role as the caterer.

But Queenie's raid on the chicken yard didn't end there. The owner of the prize poultry suspected wrongly that the unsexed bitch was a fully endowed female, on which taxes were then higher than on a spayed animal. He therefore haled Queenie's mistress into court on a charge that she was defrauding the city treasurer by passing off her pet as an unsexed female.

On the day of the trial the courtroom was jammed, and when the time came for Queenie's mistress to appear in the dock, the judge expressed his dismay that a woman of her standing would attempt to palm off an unaltered bitch for a spayed animal in order to save a few pennies. At that juncture, Queenie's owner put her two right forefingers between her lips and blew a shrill whistle, after which her pet, who had accompanied her to court, loped down the aisle to the judge's bench.

With the stage set for a confrontation, Queenie's mistress yanked up her dog's tail, revealing her private parts. She then remarked dryly, "If your honor will step down here and inspect Queenie's posterior, you'll see the scars where the veterinary sewed her up." After that, she wheeled on the spectators and demanded, "Now I ask you, doesn't that prove that Queenie is a perfect lady?"

13. Offbeat Advocates Relieved Legal Boredom

Like any other Southern town, the Queensport of my youth had a bumper crop of lawyers, varying in qualifications from a few fairly honest attorneys at the top of the legal ladder to hordes of money-grubbing shysters on the lowest rung. None of these need detain us, however, for it will be the offbeat Queensport advocates rather than the pillars of justice or the pettifoggers who will be highlighted here.

One of these mavericks, a legal Lazarus who lived off the crumbs from the more prosperous lawyers' tables, augmented his sketchy practice by operating a newsstand near the building in which the offices of Queensport's more prestigious attorneys were located. This character, who also had political ambitions, had run for every municipal job from dogcatcher to councilman in his time, always being roundly trounced at the polls. Even so, he never gave up, and on one occasion he announced his candidacy for mayor. This proved a little too ambitious, however, and he was finally persuaded by his cronies to take his name off the ballot.

On the day he reached that decision, a witty Queensport attorney stopped at his newsstand to buy a copy of the afternoon paper. It so happened the customer's brother was also running for mayor, so the news vendor thought it would be a good opportunity to announce his retreat from the political arena. Assuming a grandiloquent stance, he addressed his customer.

" . . . *grabbed up a hefty chamber pot . . .* "

"Will you give your brother an important message from me?" he demanded.

"Certainly," the legal wit replied.

"Well, tell him I've withdrawn," the recent aspirant for mayor announced grandly.

There was a brief pause, then the mayoral candidate's brother quipped, "May I add it's a pity your father didn't do likewise!"

Another shady Queensport lawyer maintained an office on the second floor of a building directly opposite the city's railroad depot. Not only were his name and calling emblazoned in bold gold letters on the window of his office, he used another and less professional method to drum up trade. Placed prominently on the windowsill beside his desk was a big red-paper, brassbound cheerleader's megaphone which he used regularly to call attention to his services.

With the arrival of each incoming trainload of passengers from the surrounding country, some of them presumably in need of legal advice, he would stand at the open window and bellow "Need a lawyer?" through his horn to the crowd surging out of the station. If anyone fell for his sales pitch, he would yell, "Meet you in a minute," after which he would throw down the megaphone and rush down the stairs in order to lead the unwary lamb to the slaughter.

There was also a team of Queensport lawyers, one an alcoholic, the other a teetotaler, who were hired on one occasion to inventory the worldly goods of a widow before her husband's estate could be settled. The inventorying, done by the alcoholic, looked like a competent job until the non-drinking partner neared the end of the document. The appraiser had apparently begun his work in cold sobriety, for everything was set down in order - the living room furniture, bedroom furnishings, kitchen utensils, linen, silver, and dining room fittings - until the sideboard was reached. Then the next three entries made the teetotaling partner open his eyes a little wider.

Right after the sideboard was listed, the appraiser put down "One pint of fine old whiskey, full." This was followed by "One pint of damned good whiskey, partially full," finally ending with "One damned whiskey bottle, empty!" The next entry on the inventory lifted the curtain on what had occurred. It read, "Two revolving oriental rugs!"

Still another Queensport legal practitioner was in the habit of going on periodic benders, usually winding up some place far from home. Once when he was on one of these alcoholic peregrinations he came to sufficiently to realize he was in New York City but was unable to recall the name of the hotel into which he had checked. In that desperate state he telephoned one of his aunts, a Queensport schoolteacher, long after midnight. When she answered the telephone she recognized the considerably fuzzy voice of her nephew at the other end.

"What in God's name are you calling me for at this hour?" she demanded querulously.

Disregarding the question, the drunk countered with "Say, auntie, how about helping me out of a hole?"

"What kind of a hole?" the aunt asked warily.

"Well, here I am in New York City, and I need some information," he hiccupped.

"What sort of information?" she inquired.

"Well, it's like this," the drunk continued. "What was the name of the general who beat the hell out of Napoleon at Waterloo?"

"It was the Duke of Wellington," the aunt replied, hardly able to conceal her impatience. "But what has that got to do with your problem?"

"By God, that's it! It's the Hotel Wellington!" the drunk trumpeted, adding, "You've saved the day, auntie! I've been staggering around New York ever since the bars closed trying to remember the name of the hotel, and all I could come up with was Waterloo and I knew damned well that wasn't right. Then I realized if I could get you on the line, you'd come up with the answer!" Following another hiccup, the drunk called out cheerily, "Thanks a million, auntie!" after which he hallooed, "The Wellington! Tally ho!"

There was still another Queensport lawyer who was notorious for his usurious practices. When he died the members of his family were so delighted with their sizeable legacies they speedily erected a tall granite obelisk over his remains. That didn't please one of his victims, however, for those who made a pilgrimage to the cemetery to admire the imposing monolith the Sunday after it was set up were greeted with an extra four-line epitaph scribbled on the monument's base with indelible pencil. It read:

> Here lies confound old ten percent,
> The longer he lived, the less he spent.
> He robbed the poor, and he robbed the rich;
> New he's fleecing the Devil, the son of a bitch!

Perhaps the most notable eccentric of the Queensport bar, however, was a character nicknamed "Stonewall," whose personal peculiarities far outstripped his legal abilities. Stonewall's unusual moniker had been earned over the years by his unswerving devotion to The Lost Cause, the failure of which he attributed to Great Britain's refusal to acknowledge the Confederacy.

As a rule, even the most dyed-in-the-wool Queensport disciples of Dixie laughed at Stonewall's tirades, but on one occasion his pointed remarks resulted in an injury to his shiny receding forehead, the long red scar from which he carried to his grave. While taking a cruise on a coastal steamer, Stonewall was loudly berating Queen Victoria to a drinking crony for her apparent indifference to the internecine struggle of 1861-65 when he was interrupted by a thunderous rap on his stateroom door.

Opening up, Stonewall was confronted by a militant, tweedy British female journalist who was touring the United States and who happened to occupy the next cabin. At that juncture, according to Stonewall's drinking buddy, the following exchange took place.

"Are you the blackguard who has been defaming my queen?" the woman demanded angrily.

"To Hell with your damned queen as well as the whole Goddamned British Empire!" Stonewall shot back.

With that added insult ringing in her ears, the irate lady reporter grabbed up a hefty chamber pot and broke it over Stonewall's head.

According to fairly reliable Queensport gossip, Stonewall took his ant-British sentiments so far he would not play poker because the game contained a royal flush. Chit-chat also reported he even refused to use Prince Albert smoking tobacco because it was named for Albert Edward, Queen Victoria's eldest son. Rumor also whispered he would not permit Lipton's tea to be served in his home because the company was owned by a British peer. Tittle-tattle also reported that his long-suffering wife had to take a sniff of ordinary household ammonia when she felt the vapors coming on instead of a whiff of smelling salts, because the popular brand then in vogue with the upper-class Queensport ladies bore the regal trade name of Crown Lavender.

Even so, Stonewall put up a brave fight against Britannia until almost the end of his life, when an unexpected blow shattered him completely. When his daughter had a yen to join the Patriots and investigated the family tree, she discovered that her paternal ancestors had all been uncompromising Tories at the time of Concord, Lexington and Yorktown. That did it! Queensport's former roaring anti-lion went out like a lamb!

Then there was the Queensport legal practitioner whose life history supported the old adage that he who laughs last, laughs best. The old fellow had been a familiar figure for half a century in the town's legal circles, where he was more or less taken for granted by his more prosperous associates. Having graduated with honors from Mr. Jefferson's university before The Late Unpleasantness, he had returned home, hung out his shingle, and was building up a lucrative practice when the bombardment of Fort Sumter put a temporary stop to his legal career. Four years later he returned to Queensport and tried to begin all over again, but success eluded him at every turn.

Tradition said an unhappy marriage and an increasing fondness for the bottle were the principal causes. Be that as it may, it was not long before he had ceased to have an office of his own, and for the remaining years of his active practice he had to be content to do hack jobs for the more thriving lawyers of the community, many of whom were unprincipled scoundrels. Finally, when he could work no longer and it was almost certain that he would end his days in the poorhouse, he devised a scheme that successfully kept him well provided for during his remaining years.

The plan was quite simple. Throughout his lifetime the old fellow had acquired an encyclopedic knowledge of the shady practices of many of his still active legal confreres that were best left untold. Using this information as a lever for blackmail, he set to work. Notifying the culprits he was devoting his leisure time to recording these episodes for posterity, it was not long before he began receiving regular cash donations and ample supplies of good whiskey to persuade him to forget the slick deals that stuck in his memory.

When he died, there was a mad scramble to his room to discover the manuscript. After a frantic search through his possessions a battered old ledger was found on the dusty top shelf of a closet in the boardinghouse room where he had passed his last comfortable years. Opening it, the searchers read: "The Facts As I Know Them," followed by his signature engrossed in a bold Spencerian hand on the flyleaf. On the next page they discovered only five words, "Ha! Ha! you gullible bastards!" written in the same elegant penmanship. The remaining pages of the thick tome were blank.

" . . . you ain't seen nothin' yet."

14. Three Alternatives to Shank's Mare

Even Queensport's former public transportation system, ranging from hacks for hire and trolley cars to the motorized jitneys, so called because five cents, popularly known as a "jit," was the price of a ride, contributed to the city's folklore. For instance, on one occasion during the horse-drawn hack era, a traveling salesman ran out of a Queensport hotel, shook the drowsy driver on the box of a waiting hack, and yelled, "Wake up, damn it! I've got to catch a train in ten minutes. If you get me to the depot on time I'll give you a silver dollar."

"My God, man," the old fellow spluttered. "My horse is so slow he couldn't catch last year's flies. He's an old, worn out cavalry horse and is just about ready to drop in his tracks."

"A cavalry horse!" the salesman exclaimed with a gleam in his eye, "Move over, Dad, and I'll show you how to drive him."

Leaping on the box, the salesman grabbed the reins and called out, "Forward, march!" The old nag pricked up his ears, switched his tail, and took off at a brisk trot for the depot. When they arrived, the salesman commanded, "Halt!" and the old horse came to an abrupt standstill. Tossing the hackman the silver dollar, the salesman made a rush for his train.

A few weeks later when another man came out of the same hotel and made a similar request, the driver said, "Hop right in, I'll get you there as quick as a cat can wink her eye." At a stentorian "Forward, march!" the old horse put on a repeat performance, but as they approached the station the hackman seemed puzzled. Turning to his passenger, he shouted, "Sorry, boss, but you'll have to leap out when I get to the depot. I've clean forgot the word to stop this Goddamned fireball!"

As for the trolley cars, there is this tale of a Queensport matron, the president of her neighborhood garden club, who rode out to a nearby beach one summer evening with a friend to attend an open-air concert. As they strolled closer to the bandstand to get a better view of the musicians, the friend noticed that her companion's attention was concentrated on some handsome geraniums growing nearby. Later, when they boarded the trolley for home, she observed the flower lover was secreting several good-sized cuttings under her summer coat.

As the trolley was crowded, both women had to stand, and the geranium admirer had some difficulty holding on to the strap with one hand while grasping the cuttings with the other. All went well until the trolley approached a dangerous bend in the track known as "Dead Man's Curve." When the car reached that stretch it lurched so violently it proved to be the geranium snatcher's downfall.

Shaken loose from her hold on the strap, the matron pawed the air wildly to stabilize herself, completely forgetting the geraniums she was trying to hide. In a moment, cuttings flew in all directions much to everyone's amusement, but that didn't faze the posey purloiner. Once she had regained her balance, she gathered up her floral loot into a bouquet. Then, turning to another straphanger, she observed archly, "They won't grow, you know, unless you steal them."

To toss in a personal recollection, one evening in the late nineteen twenties a schoolmate and I boarded a trolley after attending a movie only to discover that once we had sat down there was only one seat left on the car. The occupant of the window side of that particular brown-leather perch was a pompous military officer of some sort, resplendent in gold braid and multiple decorations. As his girth was ample, there was very little room left on the aisle side of the seat.

When the car stopped shortly afterward, an equally portly woman got on lugging a big paper flour sack, the contents of which remained unidentified for the time being. Giving the officer a hard look, she eased herself onto the narrow space beside him and then deposited the bag in the aisle. Everything went normally until the car careened around a corner, at which time the woman slipped off the slick leather seat and landed on top of the bulging paper flour sack. There was a sickening crunch, after which the woman arose and yelled, "God damn it! There goes my nine dozen eggs!"

Everyone, except the woman's former seat partner laughed, while some, I hate to say, applauded. That made the woman even more furious, and when the conductor opened the door to take on other passengers, she grabbed up the sticky mess and heaved it into the night. That would have solved the problem if no one had been in the line of fire, but just as the bag left the car, it landed in the face of a woman who was about to get aboard.

After that, the laughing attained gale force, but some kinder people in the front of the car arose to the occasion and offered their handkerchiefs to the victim to wipe the egg off her face. Meanwhile, the first woman assumed a militant stance in the aisle and aired her grievances in language that practically took the paint off the bulkhead. When she finally stalked off the car, the conductor closed the door, turned around, wiped his brow, and remarked loudly, "Whew! How would you like to be married to that one?"

In answer to that flippant observation, the other woman who had gotten the eggs in her face leaped to her feet screaming like a wounded hyena and began her own set of variations on the other woman's tirade by declaring: "Now let me tell you, you Goddamned snide bastard! . . ."

By the time we reached our stop she was doing so well we hated to leave the car. Anyway, after that enchanting slice of real life, my friend and I didn't frequent the movie palaces for some time. The silver screen would have been an anticlimax.

Turning to the jitneys, during World War I a dignified elderly Queensport matron boarded one and found herself surrounded by a group of jolly sailors. After taking her seat, she noticed the young salt sitting beside her had rolled up the sleeves of his jumper, revealing a flamboyant tattoo of the American flag on his right arm. "Young man, permit me to compliment you," the matron beamed. "That tattoo of Old Glory on your arm is certainly a striking indication of your sterling patriotism." There was a pause, after which the sailor grinned, tipped the matron a wink, and replied, "Thanks lady, but you ain't seen nuthin' yet. I'm sittin' on the Kaiser!"

Queensport's best jitney story, however, concerned one of the town's social leaders who boarded one of the cumbersome old vehicles a year or so after the Armistice and headed toward the downtown shopping district. On the way she became involved in the exchange of a juicy bit of gossip with a friend, and before she realized it she had overshot her destination. Still hoping to collect all of the details, she backed toward the front of the jitney as her friend put the final touches on the scandalous tale.

Unfortunately, just as the driver flung open the exit door, she caught one of her high heels in the hem of her dress, and before she knew what had happened, she was sprawled on the sidewalk. At that point the driver leaned out of the door and drawled, "Lady, did you fall?" Giving him a look of withering contempt, the disheveled woman shot back, "No, you stupid bastard, I always get off this way!"

15. Musical Criticism
From On High

Unless you belonged to a Queensport family whose bankroll was sufficiently opulent to enable you to study music with a testy old Italian who was deferentially referred to as "Signor" by his provincial sycophants, you had to fall back on two socially approved, but less capable, piano teachers who charged considerably less for their services. These were a dour spinster, who was also the official pianist of the Varina Howell Davis Chapter of the Southern Valkyries, or a raffish widow, a member of a down-at-the-heels family whose eccentric instruction methods came under the same category as the Peace of God which passeth all understanding.

If you drummed out scales and five-finger exercises long enough to the accompaniment of the wagging metronome of Marse Robert's vestal, you eventually wound up being able to play "Monastery Bells," "The Maiden's Prayer," or similar pianistic fodder, long on keyboard pyrotechnics but short on musical content.

With the widow, however, things were delightfully different. She espoused no particular system of study, and her pupils rarely achieved enough competence to play even the simplest tunes without committing every musical crime in the book. Even so, they had a heck of a lot of fun during the learning - or rather lack of learning - process.

Besides being a musical preceptress of questionable repute, the widow was also famous for her stentorian recitations of "The Face on the Barroom Floor" and "The

" . . . her erratically inspired Orphean space trips. . . "

Shooting of Dan Magrew," which she frequently declaimed at social gatherings with flashing eyes and flailing arms after taking a surreptitious swig of homemade peach brandy from a large medicine bottle she always carried in her reticule.

Her chef d'oeuvre, however, was a hair-raising set of variations on "Dixie" of her own composing, a ten-minute stretch of pianistic pandemonium she never performed the same way twice. Her rendition of that war-horse, liberally peppered with "hummingbird droppings" (the widow's name for grace notes), was guaranteed to make any lawn party, bazaar, or church social a success, even though the *cognoscenti* maintained that the tone-deaf executant played the right hand part in one key and the accompaniment in another. Blissfully unaware of their criticisms, the widow continued to emulate the more cacophonous moderns, and Queensport for once was avant-garde and didn't know it!

These accomplishments paled, however, before the widow's real legacy to her pupils - the unforgettable memory of her annual recitals, usually presented on warm summer evenings alive with blinking lightning bugs, in some church hall charitably donated for the occasion. Contrary to accepted custom, these musical soirees were not the usual boring renditions of pianistic morceaux by pupils who were rewarded afterward with the customary cheap gold plated lyre pins which turned green before the recipients reached home again. As the widow apparently got a belly full of her pupils' drummings throughout the year, she reversed the ritual, and when the time for the recital rolled around, she favored the public with a couple of hours of her own erratically inspired Orphean space trips for a change.

While bewildered parents sat in stunned silence, stirring up a breeze with garish fans handed out as advertisements by some local funeral parlor, and wondered what in hell was going on, the widow's pupils (of whom I was one) clustered around her and loudly applauded her pianistic renderings. And renderings was the right word, too! For by the time she had pounded out "The Midnight Fire Alarm," "The Burning of Rome," "Ben Hur's Chariot Race," and "Napoleon's Last Charge," the patient old piano she had been belaboring must have felt like one of the early Christian martyrs after a pride of famished lions had worked him over.

Unfortunately all good things eventually come to a halt, a truism I learned to my sorrow after having been a particularly ardent rooter at one of the widow's more memorable recitals. My long-suffering mother, who was beginning to seriously doubt that my musical training was profiting by such hit-or-miss instruction as the widow was capable of giving, was in the audience on that particular occasion.

After surviving that endurance contest, she gave me the choice of either giving up trying to master the complexities of "Mary's Pet Waltz," which I had been inflicting on the neighborhood for six months, or switching to the Italian professor mentioned earlier who she hoped would serve as a suitable pilot to steer me out of the musical doldrums. With the rashness of youth, always on the lookout for a peak in Darien from which to discover new experiences, I chose the latter, little realizing in doing so I was leaving my musical salad days behind me.

My new teacher was a cantankerous and myopic old tyrant with spiky salt and pepper hair that made him look like an identical twin of General Paul von Hindenburg. He was also basically dishonest, for being a fairly competent teacher he realized from the beginning of our relationship that he was wasting his efforts on anyone so musically trifling. Even so, that didn't prevent him from collecting his fee for being a temporary masochist.

Meanwhile, to make it simpler for both of us, and to continue to line his pockets, he kept me on a steady diet of musical pablum until our uneven partnership was terminated dramatically a year or so later. In the meantime, I had the opportunity to play at least once in public, after which any aspirations on my part of becoming the heir of Paderewski were literally jerked out of me by my wrathful instructor at one of his annual recitals.

These occasions were full-dress affairs and were held in the big double parlors of his home, at which time the rooms were spruced up with rented palms in tubs, while the life-sized plaster busts of Beethoven, Mozart and Chopin, which presided over our weekly lessons, were outfitted with bay leaf chaplets to make the affairs more festive. Beaming mothers in their best flowered hats occupied collapsible chairs in one room, while we pupils, under the eagle eye of our choleric teacher, squirmed nervously on other chairs near the mahogany grand piano in the other, waiting for our time to shine.

For that memorable occasion I had been giving a musical bagatelle, "The Camp of the Gypsies," by some romantic German composer, to show what I had learned. But the more I thought about it, the more I realized it was too tamely composed, and when the time came for me to perform, I threw caution to the winds.

Feeling my teacher would be powerless to stop me, I launched into the selection, but instead of playing it as it was written, I tossed in octaves and trills at random, winding up with a glittering glissando from the lowest note on the piano all the way up the keyboard. The applause was deafening, and I was secretly congratulating myself on having gotten away with musical mayhem when I felt an iron grip on my shoulder.

Then, my teacher waved for silence, after which he rasped in his heavy accent, "All right, now that you've made a jackass of yourself, let's see if you can play it the way it is really written!" Without releasing his hold, he lifted me into the air and replaced me on the piano stool where my enforced reinterpretation of the musical gypsy encampment was so tame it didn't even raise a tremble from the bay leaves encircling the plaster composers' brows.

After that fiasco, my mother grew weary of the easy but catchy pieces the professor had been assigning me and suggested it was high time that my frail technical barque was launched on the stormier seas of the classics. Under pressure, the professor gave in and provided me with a simplified version of the first movement of what a program note in a Queensport church bulletin once hilariously designated as "Beethoven's Moonshine Sonata."

I found it dreadfully dull stuff after the sprightlier rhythms of such items as "The Jolly Darkies" I had begun to enjoy pounding out on the old square grand piano at home. Nevertheless, I tried to cope with it, knowing at the same time nothing I ever did would please my mentor, who gritted his teeth every time my hands touched the keyboard.

The afternoon of my musical emancipation was hot and muggy, and I had just begun to drum out the easy adaptation of Beethoven's *"Sonata quasi una fantasia"* when a raging thunderstorm broke over the Queensport rooftops. A few moments later a bolt of lightning struck the chimney of the house in which my long-suffering teacher was patiently enduring my pianistic dereliction, sending the brass plate in front of the closed fireplace sailing across the room.

The flying object barely missed the professor and me, while the room was so filled with accumulated soot from the chimney we wound up looking like a couple of end men in a minstrel show. At that point the professor let out a bellow that would have shamed a Bull of Bashan and uttered his final criticism on my slipshod playing. "Madre de Jesu Christo!," he roared, wiping the grime from his wrinkled old face. "Even God Almighty can't stand what you're doing to Beethoven!"

16. Gags Minus Prescribed Emetics

Doctors' offices and hospital wards would seem to be the least likely places to look for gags, but you don't have to be a devotee of black humor to appreciate some of the laughable situations that occasionally occur in such surroundings. For instance, here are a couple of certified quips made by two quick-on-the-trigger Queensporters while they were undergoing routine physical checkups.

The principal in the first little farce was a genial retired Navy chief petty officer who felt the necessity for a thorough going over by his doctor. All went well until the final rectal probe, at which time the ex-chief registered extreme discomfort at the thoroughness with which the physician went about his business. Aware of his patient's physical distress, the doctor tried to ease the situation by remarking casually, "Oh, come now, you ought not to mind what I'm doing. After all, you were in the Navy for twenty years."

"Yes, I know I was," the ex-chief groaned, "but the Navy was never in me!"

On another occasion a Queensport humorist was undergoing the same exploratory treatment. Finally, when the doctor was through, the wag turned to him and inquired coyly, "Well, Doc, does this mean we're engaged?"

To give the doctors equal billing, there was this story of a witty old Queensport family practitioner who was approached by a sexually indiscreet young socialite who was anxious to learn if it was possible to have a baby in

" . . . the survival of the fittest."

less than nine months' time. There was a brief pause during which the doctor peered inquisitively over his bifocals at the young woman's tell-tale tummy. Then he replied solemnly, "Only the first one, my dear."

There was another Queensport doctor who devoted most of his vacations to visiting prehistoric sites where excavations were in progress. One of these trips took him to some place in the western part of the United States where archaeologists were unearthing the remains of several dinosaurs. The great size of the bones prevented his bringing home anything spectacular to add to his collection of antediluvian artifacts. Even so, he did manage to acquire a portable souvenir that he subsequently used to illustrate the mutability of human existence to those of his patients who were inclined to think too highly of their places in the sun.

When confronted with persons of pompous self-importance, he would slyly reach into one of the pockets of his white uniform jacket and take out an irregular brown blob resembling a misshapen rock formation. Then, after contemplating it for a few moments, he would lift his eyes to whoever was seated in his consultation chair and observe casually, "This is a fragment of fossilized dinosaur dung." After that had produced the desired shock, he would add, "Whenever I begin to have delusions of grandeur I always fondle it and reflect on the survival of the fittest."

Shifting to Queensport's hospitals, there is this yarn of a man who underwent a serious operation, after which he was moved to a room overlooking one of the city's main thoroughfares. Some time during the night when he was gradually regaining consciousness, a fire broke out in a pawn shop across the street from the hospital. When he came to sufficiently to realize what was happening he became alarmed by the lurid reflections of the flames dancing on the ceiling of his room.

Just then one of the Catholic Sisters of Charity who operated the hospital walked in to check on his condition. Catching sight of her he wailed, "Good God, Sister! I knew

I'd wind up down here, but what in Hell are you doing here?"

Then there was the tale of the handsome Queensport philanderer who was married to a very jealous wife. Just before being wheeled into the operating room of another hospital for an appendectomy, he begged his spouse to grant him one request.

"And what would that be?" she snapped.

"Well, when I come out from under the ether, promise me I'll be gazing into the face of the most beautiful nurse in the hospital."

Having no intention of providing her spouse with an excuse for further dalliance, the wife bestirred herself, and by the time he was returned to his room, she had engaged the oldest and homeliest nurse on the hospital staff. All went well until the temporarily out-of-commission Don Juan opened his eyes feebly, at which moment the white-capped crone his wife had hired leaned over him and croaked, "Anything you want, buddy?" Closing his eyes again, the man moaned, "My God! I must be in Hell!"

That truth is often stranger than fiction is also exemplified by the following Mack Sennett scenario that preceded the birth of a Queensport baby around the turn of the century. When the child's mother announced that her time had come, her husband summoned the family doctor who arrived at the couple's home shortly afterward in one of the newfangled horseless carriages.

In his haste, however, the doctor had forgotten his bag, so he asked the prospective father to use his vehicle to drive back to his office to fetch it. The expectant father had never operated an electric buggy before, but after having been shown by the doctor how to get it going, he sallied forth on his mission. Unfortunately, the briefing the doctor had given him did not include how to stop the contraption. As a result, he kept circling the block where the doctor's office was located while he frantically fumbled for what he hoped would be the cutoff gadget.

Finally, when the doctor's nurse observed that his efforts to stop in front of the building were unsuccessful, she stuck her head out of the window and asked what he wanted. When he yelled back that he had come for the doctor's bag as he sailed by again, she complicated matters by calling out, "Which one? He has three!"

On the next encirclement of the block the distraught father shouted, "Throw me the one he uses to deliver a baby!" Then he breezed off again, followed by every cur in the neighborhood yelping in full cry. The next time around the nurse was waiting on the curb with the proper bag. Snagging this as he whizzed by, the man headed for home, where he found the doctor waiting excitedly for him on the front porch.

When the latter took in the situation, he called out, "Throw it to me when you come around again. Your wife's time is getting short!" The bag was delivered on the next encirclement of the block and the doctor rushed into the house. In the meantime, the frantic father kept up his mad career with the apparently unstoppable horseless carriage.

At length, however, luck was with him, and he pulled the right lever, bringing the electric buggy to a sudden stop. Leaping out, he made a dash for home where he learned that his efforts had not been in vain. As he rushed into the house he was informed by the beaming doctor that his wife had just presented him with a bouncing girl.

". . . one of hi- hi- his disciples!"

17. Off-color Histrionics

Queensport also had its share of theatrical anecdotes, one of the best of which concerned a flighty matron who set out one day during the early nineteen-hundreds to buy a new coffee pot. The old one she had been using had lost the rivet that kept its top in place, making it perilous to use when it was filled with scalding coffee.

Hoping to cut a stylish figure in the downtown shopping area, the matron had worn a new hat, a frilly confection of starched black lace stretched over a wire frame and accented with a jet buckle and a flaring satin butterfly bow. Moisture of any kind was death to a chapeau of that sort, and as bad luck would have it, a heavy rain set in just as the matron descended from the trolley car she had taken to perform her errand.

Glancing around desperately for a dry place in which to duck to protect her hat, the woman was attracted by the sign of Queensport's first "picture show" - a blinking series of red, white and blue electric bulbs a few doors down the street. Making a dash for the nickelodeon, she bought a five cent ticket and walked into its cavernous darkness where she discovered the picture being featured was an episode in a serial having to do with an ingenue abducted by a gang of desperados who were holding her for ransom in their lair in the Rocky Mountains.

Removing her hat, the matron soon became so engrossed in the action on the screen that she was completely oblivious to the fact that she was badly manhandling her delicate millinery. Meanwhile, as the picture progressed, the bandits were shown engaged in a poker game, during which the captive miss, who had been pressed into service as a short-order cook, jerkily approached the table to supply them with coffee.

This automatically produced a stirring in the matron's memory, and when the heroine began pouring coffee into a mug, the woman, subconsciously recalling the defective coffee pot at home, leaped to her feet and shrieked: "Look out, you fool! the top'll fall off!" A moment later someone yanked open a window in the projection booth and yelled, "For Christ sake, shut up down there!" Then the window banged shut and the show continued. When the episode was over, the matron put on her by then badly mauled hat and attempted to slink out of the theater.

Fate was not kind to her, however, for as she reached the door she was confronted by the theater owner, who demanded loudly if she was "the dame who yelled out in there a few minutes ago." "Why, yes," the matron admitted, assuming what little dignity she had left. "I hope you'll forgive me."

Reaching into his pocket, the man took out a nickel and handed it to the matron. "Here, lady, take this," he barked. "And don't you ever come in here again. You're too flighty to take in picture shows!"

Much later, when Queensport had acquired its share of picture palaces, one of them was the arena for another little farce. When the movie "The Gorilla" hit Queensport, a local wag was hired to dress up in an ape costume and ride around town in an open touring car to advertise the sensational picture. His promotional efforts were not confined to the open air, however, for he also paid periodic visits to the theater when the movie was being shown, at which times the management would suddenly make his presence known by flashing a spotlight on the place where he happened to be seated.

During one of these visitations, the ersatz gorilla sat down next to a timid Queensport schoolteacher. Sensing that something large and hairy was seated beside her, the woman turned in that direction just as a lurid green spotlight was turned on the "gorilla" from the projection box. Then, just as she was about to faint, the "gorilla," recognizing the schoolteacher, reached over, patted her on the hand and growled, "Hi, Miss Em, I'm Jim Jones. Don't you remember teaching me in the first grade at Robert E. Lee School?"

Like most other American cities of that time, Queensport had its Little Theater. Even though the extramarital and other surreptitious amorous activities that went on there resulted in quite a few divorces and shotgun weddings, the hectic strivings of its dedicated amateurs went a long way toward relieving the tedium of existence.

Using an abandoned garage as a playhouse, a group made up of the more emancipated Queensport younger set, who refused to burn incense any longer at the shrine of Marse Robert, set to work. After much effort they succeeded in erecting an adequate stage equipped with a dyed monk's cloth curtain at one end of the drafty structure. At the same time an arrangement for seats was made with a local undertaker by borrowing folding chairs from his establishment for the nights on which plays were being presented.

Usually this worked out smoothly, but if a funeral service coincided with the period during which the play was being performed, the chairs had to be rounded up after the final curtain the night before the obsequies and whisked back to the mortuary in order that the bereaved might be suitably accommodated the next day.

Another embarrassing arrangement at the makeshift theater also presented a nagging problem. Lacking the wherewithal to alter the existing plumbing facilities of the former garage, the amateur thespians had to put up with a toilet occupying a prominent position just off stage, a situation that occasionally resulted in extracurricular sound effects that baffled the uninitiated in the audience during the performances.

Inevitably someone helping backstage would get an uncontrollable urge to use the john in the midst of a

passionate love scene onstage, and the temporary simu-
lated bliss of the performers would suddenly be interrupted by a flush or blast behind the scenes, much to the
delight of the irreverent on the other side of the footlights.
Eventually this kink was ironed out by the installation of
a hasp and padlock on the door of the water closet, one
of the principal duties of the props manager being the
checking on the security of the contraption before the
signal for the first curtain was buzzed.

There was one occasion, however, when the arrangement did not work out as intended. During a production
of the Victorian melodrama, "The Drunkard, or The Fal-
len Saved," the pre-performance backstage activities were
particularly frenetic. When a neighborhood bum staggered in and asked to use the toilet, someone showed him
where it was located and then completely forgot all about
him. Apparently the old fellow had imbibed too freely for
he fell asleep on the stool, and when the props manager
fastened the lock on the door he did it automatically
without checking to see if the place was occupied.

Everything went well until the old mother in the play
was dying onstage on a straw pallet in the attic of a New
York tenement, when the silence was suddenly shattered
by an offstage howl that would have done credit to the
Hound of the Baskervilles. This was followed by loud and
repeated bangings, climaxed by a rasping yell, "Git me
outta dis Goddamn hole!", an unexpected dramatic *lag-
niappe* that automatically became one of the supreme
moments of Queensport's Little Theater history.

As usual in the case of amateur theatricals, disaster
always lurked in the wings, and there was hardly a
performance when the gremlins were not present in full
force to add to the general confusion. For instance, on one
occasion when a local would-be Lynn Fontanne was
doing her stuff on stage with an equally provincial
would-be Alfred Lunt, a hot and bothered couple helping
with the props decided to make out in a dark corner
behind the scenes. Unfortunately the fastenings of the
flats at the particular point where they chose to consum-

mate their vertical lovemaking had not been tightened sufficiently. Just as the principals in the play began their big scene, the offstage couple put a little too much pressure on the insecurely fastened flat, which collapsed in a cloud of dust in the middle of the stage living room with the closely entangled but temporarily inactive backstage lovers on top of it.

Fortunately the leading lady was a quick thinker, and before the audience had time to react, she ad-libbed, "Good God! We certainly do have nosy neighbors!," adding with a flourish, "Get up from there and get the bloody hell out of my apartment!" Happily the fellow working the curtain yanked it closed at that moment, but the quip was remembered in Queensport long after the name of the play had been forgotten.

On another occasion when the company was putting on "Lady Windermere's Fan," one of the elaborately made-up male actors, attired in white tie and tails, ducked out between the acts with a few cronies to a nearby tavern for a quick pickup. It so happened the man ordinarily stuttered very badly, but once he had learned his lines the stutter disappeared as if by magic while he was on stage.

His luck didn't follow him to the watering hole, however, for as he stood there, rouged and mascaraed, sipping his highball, a drunk whore on a nearby stool caught sight of his epicene loveliness in the mirror behind the bar. Wheeling on him, she sneered contemptuously, "Gee-Zus Cry-st!", after which there was a brief pause. Then the pretty boy quipped wittily, "N-n-n-no, j-j-j-just wa-wa-wa-one of hi-hi-hi-his disciples!"

The greatest stage triumph of Queensport's Little Theater, however, was purely unintentional. The play on that occasion was a modern British comedy, the setting for the first act of which was a stately drawing room furnished with eighteenth century period pieces. As a last minute embellishment, the stage manager placed two large vases containing colorful camellias, one at each end of the mantelpiece rather than grouping them together in its center as their presence in the latter place would have interfered with an important bit of stage business.

The prompter for the performance considered herself the last word on interior decoration. Thinking the camellias would be more effective if they were massed in the center of the mantel, she moved them there. When the stage manager (who loathed the prompter, by the way) discovered the change, he shifted the camellias back to their former position. A few moments later, the prompter again took advantage of his absence on stage and moved the camellias back to the center of the mantel. When this was observed by the stage manager from the wings, he rushed onstage, grabbed a vase in each hand and moved them back again.

The play was scheduled to begin with no one on stage and the signal had been given for the curtain to be parted. Unaware that this had been done, the furious stage manager confronted the prompter and bellowed, "Look here, you Goddamn busybody, there's a good reason why these flowers should be at the ends rather than in the center of that mantel, and if you move them again I'll stick them up where you can't put a plaster!" This gratuitous scene elicited a wild outburst of applause from the delighted audience, but that didn't end the affair.

The next morning the drama critic for the Queensport *Courier* began his review of the play thus: "The current attraction at Queensport's Little Theater isn't worth a damn, but if the stage manager and the prompter for the performance can be persuaded to repeat last night's impromptu prologue for the rest of its run, it will be worth the price of a season ticket!"

18. Death Wore a Tragicomic Mask

Even Death formerly wore a tragicomic mask in Queensport's more select circles. If you were anyone beginning with a capital A (and that ran the gamut downward from the well-heeled to the impecunious of certified Confederate ancestry) there was only one approved funeral director who could possibly be entrusted with the last and sometimes hilarious rites.

For snobbish reasons, the gray suede gloves, ascot ties, cutaway coats, striped trousers, spats and patent leather shoes of the attendants of his establishment were deemed more acceptable than the everyday garb worn by the employees of the less prestigious undertakers who catered to those not belonging to the socially elect. Also, the hearses of the favored establishment—subdued black for the middle-aged and above, dove gray for those under forty or those reluctant to reveal their ages, and snow white for children and presumably virginal adult females of all ages—seemed to lend a greater distinction to the last earthly outing of the deceased.

It should also be noted that the "family parlor" adjoining the "slumber room" of the preferred mortuary was provided with several copies of the one book which was also included in every respectable Queensport family library. This volume - "Famous Sons and Daughters of the Southland" - elaborately bound in black leather with gilt edges, was thoughtfully provided for those who came to view the remains but were not too grief-stricken to sample the derring-do of those who had fought with

"You left out one . . . "

Marse Robert or who had remained at home reputedly to protect the family silver from thieving Yankees.

Further, if you belonged to Queensport's elite, it was an unwritten law that your obituary must appear first in the *Courier*, the town's most prestigious and conservative morning newspaper, rather than in the *Bugle*, the afternoon journal which catered to the masses. Even so, families had to be secretive to insure that this protocol was observed, for the *Bugle*'s "body snatcher," as its obituary editor was referred to by his rival on the *Courier*, was constantly on the alert. If the news of the death of a prominent citizen leaked out before the afternoon paper's deadline, the hoped-for impact in the *Courier*'s obituary column the next morning lost much of its fizz.

As a provincial Southern newspaper, Queensport's morning journal had an indigenously ornate style, but the editors usually pruned away the more baroque prose of carried-away reporters before it appeared in print. With obituaries, however, every verbal stop was pulled out in order that the final tribute would not fall short of the elaborate floral offerings provided by the friends of the deceased.

Usually the family was so pleased with the results they ordered extra copies of the paper in order that the rhetorical eulogy might be preserved for posterity. But there was one occasion when the *Courier* really dropped the ball.

When an elderly, ancestor-conscious spinster died and a friend telephoned in the details, her obituary was highlighted with a list of twenty-two memberships she had held in local, national and international patriotic and genealogical societies. These ranged from such well-known organizations as the Founders, Patriots and the Southern Valkyries to such esoteric groups as the Descendants of the Barons of the Norman Conquest, Offshoots of the Longbows of Crecy and Agincourt, and the Progeny of Boadicea, Queen of the Iceni.

Preening himself on how pleased the surviving sister of the deceased would be with the journalistic paean he had composed, the *Courier*'s obituary editor waited a few days and then telephoned her, hoping for a compliment. He didn't get it, for when he asked the survivor how she liked what he had written, there was an ominous pause. Then she croaked, "You left out one. . .the Descendants of the Illegitimate Sons and Daughters of the Sovereigns of England, Scotland, Ireland and Wales."

In pre-radio and pre-television Queensport, funerals were regarded by many as social get-togethers rather than occasions for paying final tributes to the deceased by hovering briefly over their coffins and mumbling, "Oh, doesn't he (or she) look natural!" As the older women in my family were all compulsive funeral-goers (principally for the gossip they garnered on those occasions) I attended quite a few affairs of the sort as their interested escort and learned a lot about elemental snobbery in the process.

For instance, in my youth death was always advertised in Queensport by the tacking up of what was known as a crape (a confection of ribbon and natural or wax flowers) on the doorjamb of the home of the deceased. If you were "T.D." (i.e., "Top Drawer"), the prestigious funeral home's arcane way of designating that the corpse was rated first class socially, this was replaced with an arrangement of gilded wire shaped like the heavenly portals and known euphemistically as a "Gates Ajar."

Outfitted with a stuffed white dove suspended over the wire gateway with a ribbon in its beak bearing the initials of the departed in gold paper letters, the "Gates Ajar" refinement on the simpler crape idea was an indication of the privileged position of the deceased.

For ordinary funerals, almost any kind of tune, provided it was suitably doleful, was sufficient to fill the bill. But if the departed had been a member of the elect, the services of an organist with a fondness for the tremulous vox humana stop was deemed a necessity, while his or her renditions of "The Lost Chord," "The Holy City," or "The Last Hope" were guaranteed to wilt the emotions of even the most stoical mourner.

If that didn't do the trick, there was always the intimidating presence of the owner of the favored establishment who presided with owl-like solemnity at the door of the church or wherever the last rites were held. His whispered admonition, "Beyond the smiling and the weeping we shall be soon," as he pressed the incoming mourners' hands, was guaranteed to reduce even those who had come out of curiosity to soulful reflections before they had been ushered to their seats.

Amusing things have an eerie way of happening unexpectedly at funerals and Queensport had its share of such tales, one of the best of which concerned a portly elderly matron of the mid-Victorian era who was inevitably late to the home obsequies which were the rule at that time. On the occasion of the anecdote, the woman slunk into a house of mourning where the funeral was already in progress. Hoping not to be noticed, she sat down on what was then called a "fancy chair" in the hallway only to get the surprise of her life when a hidden music box in the seat responded to the pressure of her ample buttocks and gave forth with a spirited tinkling rendition of "Turkey in the Straw!"

Although the majority of Queensport funerals were routine, there was one which stands out in my memory as a truly outstanding performance. The deceased was a matron who had left the area when she was a bride to reside in the North where her husband was a wealthy manufacturer. When she died many years later, however, she left explicit instructions for her body to be brought back to Queensport for burial. Since she came from an adamantly unreconstructed family, the roster of those who attended her last rites in the city's principal Episcopal church was a Who's Who of latter-day Queensport Yankee haters.

During the first part of the service the proper prayers were read while a suitable number of dolorous tunes were played to lend solemnity to the occasion. After the last amen echoed from the rafters, however, an incident (planned secretly well in advance by the deceased) occurred that made every diehard Southerner present want to hop on the next train for Charleston, South Carolina, to fire on Fort Sumter and begin the War for Southern Independence all over again.

As the coffin was being wheeled down the aisle on its way to be taken to the cemetery there was a sudden dramatic pause, at which time a funeral attendant whisked off the heavy pall of American Beauty roses and smilax that had decorated it during the earlier part of the service and replaced it with the Stars and Bars.

At that point the organist halted in the midst of Handel's "Largo" and swung into a rip-roaring rendition of "Dixie." The effect was so theatrically effective that one mourner sobbed loudly, "That'll send her right into General Lee's enfolding arms!"

Back then people were always "breaking down" at funerals, an expression that conjured up visions of a stalled Model-T Ford on a muddy country road in my youthful imagination until I learned it meant the loss of control on the part of the bereaved. For those emergencies an undertaker's assistant was usually handy with a vial of smelling salts, but occasionally a friend of the family did the honors, usually with some unforseen result.

For instance, one Queensport woman always carried a small bottle of household ammonia in her reticule against such contingencies, and on one occasion when the prissy widow of a prominent citizen fainted at the grave, the concerned old biddy rushed forward, drenched her handkerchief with ammonia, and thrust in under the widow's nose. The latter's loud expostulation, "What the hell! That Goddamned stuff came near knocking the top of my head off!" when she came to was the sensational Queensport funeral utterance of the season. Even so, I recall another funeral pronouncement that topped that one.

A sprightly Queensport matron during her lifetime attracted many admirers with her wit and cleverness, but her sharp tongue and domineering disposition bruised quite a few egos. Finally, when her time came, one of the victims evened the score with a vengeance. The woman's favorite poem was Tennyson's "Crossing the Bar," which the family asked the minister to read aloud at the graveside. The cemetery was crowded for the last rites and when the gentleman of the cloth got through with the regular committal he launched into an unctuous recital of the well-known Victorian chestnut. Everything proceeded smoothly until he finished reading the last two lines:

> I hope to see my Pilot face to face
> When I have crossed the bar.

There was a pause, then someone in the crowd cleared his throat and pronounced the woman's verbal epitaph. "My God!," he exclaimed loudly, "I shudder to think of that confrontation!"

George Holbert Tucker was born in the Berkley section of Norfolk, Virginia, on September 14, 1909. He began writing features for Norfolk's *Virginian-Pilot* newspaper in 1947, and his "Tidewater Landfalls" was a popular column from its inception until Mr. Tucker's retirement from the newspaper in 1976. Two previous collections of his columns have been published, tales of growing up and coming of age in the South in the first half of the 20th century. Mr. Tucker is the author of the critically acclaimed *A Goodly Heritage: A History of Jane Austen's Family* (1983) and contributed several articles to *The Jane Austen Companion (1986)*. He presently writes a weekly column on Virginiana in the Sunday *Virginian-Pilot/Ledger-Star*. A collection of the latter, *Cavalier Saints and Sinners: Virginia History Through a Keyhole,* was published in 1990.